The Gartley Trading Method

The Gartley Trading Method

*New Techniques to Profit from the Market's
Most Powerful Formation*

ROSS L. BECK, FCSI

WILEY

John Wiley & Sons, Inc.

Published by John Wiley & Sons, Inc., Hoboken, New Jersey.
Published simultaneously in Canada.

For general information on our other products and services or for technical support, please contact our Customer Care Department within the United States at (800) 762-2974, outside the United States at (317) 572-3993 or fax (317) 572-4002.

Wiley also publishes its books in a variety of electronic formats. Some content that appears in print may not be available in electronic books. For more information about Wiley products, visit our Web site at www.wiley.com.

Library of Congress Cataloging-in-Publication Data:

Beck, Ross L., 1964–
    The Gartley trading method : new techniques to profit from the market's most powerful formation /
Ross L. Beck.
        p. cm. – (Wiley trading series)
    Includes bibliographical references and index.
    ISBN 978-0-470-58354-8
    1. Investments–Psychological aspects.   2. Investments–Decision making.   3. Gartley, H. M.   I. Title.
    HG4515.15.B43 2010
    332.63′2042–dc22

                                                                                                2010015532

Printed in the United States of America

10   9   8   7   6   5   4   3   2   1

This book is dedicated to the Creator of the Universe whose name יהדה was the subject of W.D. Gann's final book, "The Magic Word."

Contents

Foreword

Ross Beck has done a splendid job describing one of the most logical and consistent patterns when trading any market whether it be stocks, bonds, commodities, or forex. Mr. Beck explains in detail how a Gartley Pattern is formed and also integrates part of the Elliott Wave principle in conjunction with the Gartley Pattern. I would think that H.M. Gartley would be proud of the effort and detail Mr. Beck conveys to his readers.

H.M. Gartley's book, *Profits in the Stock Market*, was published in 1935—in the middle of the Great Depression—and sold at the incredible price of $1,500, roughly equivalent at the time to the price of three new Ford automobiles. To my mind, that was a small price to pay as the Gartley insights into the market are worth far more than three new cars.

In his book, Gartley described a chart pattern that we now call the AB = CD pattern. The pattern illustrated how the market will rally in an uptrend and then retrace; rally again and retrace again. The second rally forms an up-sloping parallel channel, making the overall pattern look something like a lightning bolt.

The AB=CD pattern is found in all markets and all time frames. The pattern is the foundation of Gartley buy and sell patterns and is also an integral part of other market patterns. Importantly, the pattern is a measured move where the CD leg should be similar in length to the AB leg, although sometimes the CD leg will extend. There are other rules regarding interpretation and structure that readers should endeavor to understand before attempting to trade the patterns.

Mr. Beck's book is noteworthy in that it provides excellent examples of the patterns and how to best use money management principles that are so important to becoming a consistently profitable trader. Personally, I think Mr. Beck has produced an important piece of trading history that will help anyone in need of a methodology that is consistently profitable over any time frame! I know nothing can make an author happier than presenting something that can change lives for the better.

Mr. Beck's book is part of a larger area of financial market study, market geometry, which began in the 1930s with the work of W.D. Gann. Gann became famous for the use of Gann angles, which are now found in many charting software packages. Another important but often overlooked market technician was George Bayer who wrote a book called *The Egg of Columbus*, which once sold for $25,000 in the mid-1980s. The book described the progression of Fibonacci series using diagrams of birds, fish, and mammals as a type of mystical code that has parallels to the financial markets.

One unique interest Gann and Bayer shared was an interest in cycles. It is worth noting in an article by Lisa Burrell in the *Harvard Business Review* of November 2006 that cites research by Ilia D. Dichev and Troy D. Janes into stock prices during the 28.5 day cycle between a new moon and a full moon. The article states the cycles may have application to predicting stock prices.

This is not at all surprising, given that markets are fueled by the energy of market participants. Changes in peoples' moods and behavior around moon cycles have been well documented throughout the years. And, of course, investor moods and emotions play a huge role in price behavior in the markets.

Finally, we should mention Bryce Gilmore of Australia—in many ways the father of contemporary market geometry—and author of the book *Geometry of Markets*. All of us owe Bryce a great deal of gratitude for discovering market geometry in the same manner that Gartley shared his discovery of the Gartley Pattern.

Mr. Beck's book is a worthy addition to the long line of technical analysts and their books that have helped to unlock the secrets of the financial markets.

Larry Pesavento

Preface

Many successful traders around the world agree that there are distinct patterns that repeat in the financial markets. Each trader has a favorite—head and shoulders, Elliott Wave, and so on. However, you have to ask yourself, Are some of these patterns more reliable than others?

In *The Gartley Trading Method*, I will prove to you beyond any doubt that the Gartley Pattern is the mother of all trading patterns.

As a professional derivatives trader, I have been using the Gartley method for over a decade. I will begin our discussion with an explanation of the foundation laid by H.M. Gartley in his classic book *Profits in the Stock Market*. This discussion will be followed with a description of the historical evolution of the Gartley Pattern over the decades and uncover a dimension of the setup that has been overlooked for over 70 years.

Elliott Wave traders will be relieved to find out that Elliott Wave counts don't matter anymore if you simply look for Gartley Patterns. In addition, you will learn how the original Gartley Pattern is actually a trade setup to trade Wave 3. Gann traders will be happy to read the information on W.D. Gann's mystical emblem of the circle, square, and triangle symbol in Appendix B. Is the secret of this symbol finally unlocked?

After studying many books on technical analysis, I often noticed how often the techniques they presented almost overlap each other, yet I couldn't seem to logically describe these similarities and put them to practical use for trading. I call the Gartley Pattern the missing link of technical analysis, because it is the mortar that binds most of the technical disciplines together. As you will see in Part Two, the Gartley Pattern fits within the context of most of the common classical trading patterns. In this sense, the pattern can be described as an "all-purpose" pattern. As with most patterns, it is a pattern that represents the psychology of the participants and therefore can be used on most liquid markets and most time frames.

It is my solemn responsibility as one human being to another to try to save you from yourself. If you continue to read this book, it will require you to undertake a vigorous self-examination to determine whether you should enter the trading arena. I will not make the occupation of trading look glamorous and a surefire way to get rich. It can be one of the most brutal and at times nauseating occupations of all time. Yet, if you have what it takes, you *might* be rewarded handsomely. If you don't have what it takes, that's OK, just admit it and stop fooling yourself and others. Admission is the first step of any twelve-step program. If you admit that you are more of a gambler than a trader, then return this book and buy one that will teach you how to count cards.

This book is more objective that a lot of the rather sensational material available in the trading field. It reminds me of the muscle magazines I would read as a teenager. It didn't matter how many protein shakes I drank, supplements I took, or workouts I did. I could never come close to looking like the behemoths in the magazine advertisements. I really *wanted to believe* that there was a new scientific breakthrough that would allow me to purchase a supplement to give me the body of a Mr. Olympia competitor. But is that realistic? No. The realistic part of competitive bodybuilding has more to do with the illegal use and abuse of anabolic steroids, a subject avoided by most of the sponsors of bodybuilding competitions and magazines. So it is with trading advertisements that make unrealistic claims. Remember the poster behind Mulder's desk in *The X-Files*? It had a picture of a flying saucer with the caption, "I want to believe."

I will not teach you any technical method that I have not used myself. In my quest for the holy grail, I have rediscovered a pattern that, has served me well over the years. Some may ask, If it is that good, why don't you keep it to yourself and not share it? That is a good question and should be asked of anyone who is selling you *anything* to do with trading. Remember the movie *Back to the Future 2*? The character Biff obtained a sports book with the final scores of sporting events that were going to happen in the future. He quickly started placing bets on future events and became fabulously wealthy. In a similar vein, we may fantasize about having tomorrow's *Wall Street Journal* today. I'm sure we could all agree that we could become rich with such information.

However, the more important point that I'm trying to make is this: Is it possible to lose money trading with tomorrow's *Wall Street Journal?* Yes! Have you ever had the experience of putting a trade on perfectly, where it instantly started to make money, only to watch it over subsequent days turn into a loss? In view of the foregoing, it is a certainty that someone can have the best trade setups on the planet, the proverbial "holy grail," and still lose money. Why? As we all know, the entry is only half (or less) of the equation. Trading is not just about good entry signals, it's about good entry signals combined with even better exit strategies. Trade management is crucial and it wasn't until I combined the best trade setup (the Gartley trading method) with proper exit strategies that I was able to make the Gartley Pattern work as part of a comprehensive trading system. A quick, cursory look for Gartley Pattern setups on a chart may lead someone to quickly write off the Gartley as a viable way to make money trading. However, as we will see in Part Three, "Application," with proper money management, we can make a good system great, or turn a potential losing trade into a winner with sound money management principles.

Novice to expert traders should be able to glean something from *The Gartley Trading Method*, which has as one of its main messages "Do more of what works and less of what doesn't." After reading *The Gartley Trading Method*, you will start to question all that you ever knew about technical patterns, and you will learn a comprehensive trading method, from start to finish, based on natural law and timeless principles.

Acknowledgments

First, I would like to thank my mom and my loving wife Lindsay—thanks for your patience, Zeeta! Next, my children Ceara, Hadrian, Aisha, and Trajan (aka Cearup, Gin, Lala and Purple Fish)—I will always love you. In addition, I must thank the legendary technicians who were not afraid to introduce original thought: W.D. Gann, H.M. Gartley, and William Garret. Further, I must acknowledge those market geometers still with us: Michael Jenkins, Robert Miner, and Larry Pesavento, along with special thanks to Bryce Gilmore for pioneering the use of modern market geometry for the twenty-first century! Last, but not least, I must thank Mathew and the boys at Market Analyst; Nikki and Cody at Lambert Gann; and Kate, Kevin, Meg, and Michael at John Wiley & Sons.

PART I

Foundations

Because this book has been designed for traders at all levels as an exhaustive reference about the Gartley Pattern, we will first provide beginners with some basic technical analysis in Part One, "Foundations." This section focuses on the technical methods that will be employed later on to allow us to identify high-probability Gartley Patterns. Some veteran traders will still enjoy Part One as we will be discussing some methods that they might have taken for granted, but these will be covered in the context of the Gartley Trading Method. You might find that this section fills in the gaps of your technical knowledge. Remember, a review of the basics may help you, regardless of how good you are at your occupation. Apparently Tiger Woods will often play an additional nine holes even when he wins a tournament, just to stay sharp (at least that is what he tells his wife).

Trading Myths and Reality

B efore we can progress beyond the neophyte level, we must establish a foundation of trading knowledge based on reality. In Chapter 1 we answer such questions as What is a trader? What is trading success? Is trading gambling? Do I need a computer?

WHAT IS A TRADER?

The common definition of a trader is someone who buys or sells financial instruments with the intention of realizing a profit. Examples of these financial instruments are equities, options, futures, and Forex (foreign exchange). As mentioned in the preface, H.M. Gartley wrote a book in 1935 entitled *Profits in the Stock Market*. In it, Gartley stated, "The average reader should leave the stock market alone." Gartley's statement is correct; some of us honestly have no business trading as we may be confusing speculating with gambling. (More on this will follow.)

Let's first discuss what trading is not. Some of us might think that trading is glamorous—trading floors, posh offices in Manhattan, high-end suits, limousines, and more. If you have traded, you know that this is not what trading typically looks like. It looks more like an individual who works out of his house, doesn't get enough sunlight, lacks personal hygiene, and has dirty dishes and half-empty coffee mugs stacked up on his desk beside his computer. And what about the professional trader's official uniform? Is it a brightly colored jacket from the Chicago Board of Trade? No; most traders get through the work day in a bathrobe that hasn't been washed in a while!

What are the character traits of a professional trader? A trader is someone with determination, dedication, patience, humility, perseverance, balance, contentment,

3

dedication, passion, and a commitment to lifelong education of the financial markets. What? Contentment? Humility? I want to be like the proud Gordon Gecko of the movie *Wall Street* who said, "Greed is good!" Maybe you've heard the saying, "Bulls make money, bears make money, pigs get slaughtered." If you are a greedy pig when it comes to trading or anything else in your life, you will never be happy. A Buddhist student of mine once told me that we have to be happy and content with *nothing* in order to realize that everything else in life is a bonus. If you can manifest this attitude in life, including trading, you will be much happier than a greedy pig. Remember that the rich J.P. Getty once stated, "Money does not lead to happiness—if anything, unhappiness."

Often students ask me what book they should read to learn how to trade. I would have to agree with the late W.D. Gann and say *The Holy Bible*. All of the principles required to make one a successful trader can be found in the Bible. Humility may be the foremost quality required for trading. Why? A humble man knows he *will* make mistakes, expects them, embraces them, learns from them, and then makes fewer mistakes going forward. An arrogant man thinks he is perfect, takes his losses personally, pretends that the losses didn't happen, doesn't learn from his mistakes, and is doomed to repeat them.

In Jack Schwager's *Market Wizards*, the common theme of the great traders is that at some time they all have "blown up" or experienced a loss of most of their trading capital. It almost seems like a prerequisite to becoming a legend! However, there seems to be a common attitude that precedes their eventual collapse—pride and overconfidence. King Solomon's proverb states in effect that "pride comes before a crash." This could not be more true than when it applies to trading. Pride is our Achilles heel.

Whenever we have a string of wins, it is our nature to believe that we are "special" or that we have "a gift." We rationalize that we have finally matured as traders and that maybe we were a bit too cautious prior to our newfound epiphany. At this point, we may be more inclined to relax and simply use our natural ability more than the statistical models we may have been using previously. Then something happens; we lose, not just once, but quite a few times in a row. After blowing your horn in front of your trading colleagues about your market wizardry, you may be inclined to have the gambler's mentality of "getting back to breakeven" to heal your injured ego. We now take our losses personally and have a need to prove to everyone, including ourselves, that we are still a trading god. Does this sound like a humble person? Bottom line, be humble. You will still get hurt trading, but not as badly as the arrogant, greedy, trading pig.

PULLING THE TRIGGER

Another important aspect, often overlooked in trading, is the ability to make a decision. More importantly, once we have made a decision, we have to take responsibility for it even if it's wrong; we can't play the "blame game." If you are an indecisive person, then trading will be more difficult for you than for the average person. How do I know this? I have ADD (attention deficit disorder)!

After performing his analysis, a trader ultimately needs to make a trading decision on his own. Many new traders don't relish this idea and find themselves unable to "pull the trigger." Why? Because they are worried that they might be "wrong," and due to an inflated ego, they can't admit that they are capable of making a mistake. One point they forget is that it is not about being right or wrong, it's about making money. Does anyone like to be wrong? Of course not, especially someone who has a big ego. No one ever questions your ability to make a good trading decision when you are right, when you are making money hand over fist. However, what if you make a trading decision and you are dead wrong and have lost a substantial amount of money? Do you step up to the plate and say, "Yes, that horrible trade—it was all me!" Isn't it easier to have a scapegoat standing by, ready to blame for your bad trading decision?

Ask Nick Leeson, who put all his bad trades into a hidden account that Barings Bank didn't know about (there's another movie you should watch: *Rogue Trader*). You might be "pulling a Nick" if you have to keep a convenient scapegoat around to blame for your poor trading decisions. "It was the fault of the broker, the newsletter writer, the software, God, my spouse, the stars," we might lament, but really, whose fault was it? One of the reasons Ayn Rand glorified the trader in *Atlas Shrugged* is that his success was self made. Trading decisions should not involve anyone else; they are yours only.

So a professional trader is someone who can "pull the trigger" and make a trading decision. If it doesn't work, he accepts it, learns from it, and moves on. He learns from his mistakes. We typically don't learn much from a winning trade, because the trade probably worked out the way we thought it would. It's usually when we have a loser that we can learn. But, unfortunately, it's human nature to avoid painful situations including the recollection of a trading loss. We have a tendency to want to bury our heads in the sand. The classic broker response to a client that has lost money is, "Let's win it back!" This appeals to many neophyte traders because they instinctively choose to ignore the loss (pain) and quickly make up for it (pleasure) by hastily putting on another trade. This is like going from the frying pan into the fire. The trader in this example had probably spent a lot of time with his analysis to do the first trade. After suffering a loss, he is typically not going to spend as much time with his analysis on the next "let's win it back" trade. How do you think that is going to work?

TRADING VERSUS GAMBLING

H.M. Gartley wrote in *Profits in the Stock Market*, "Unfortunately for most dabblers in Wall Street, the gambling approach is most often used. The reason is simple. The average person is too often governed first by downright laziness, and secondly by the silly desire to gain something for nothing."

Most define gambling as placing a wager on an uncertain event with a monetary result (win or lose) in a short period of time. Ultimately, the choice is yours. Will you spend the time necessary to learn how to achieve a trading edge? Or will you be lazy? H.M. Gartley made the following observation in his book *Profits in the Stock Market*:

> It is a sad commentary upon human nature that so many individuals go into the stock market with surplus funds which have required considerable effort to amass, and assume the risk of stock trading, which is far greater than in ordinary business, with only a fraction of the knowledge which they would expect to employ on the business or profession in which they make their living. This is why stock trading, for most people, is gambling, rather than speculating.

If you haven't seen the movie *21*, please do so. You will see that though someone might be playing a table game in a casino, it doesn't mean he is gambling. The movie is the true story of MIT students who applied a system to blackjack that would give them an advantage over the house. They spent months and months of practice on their system; the fact that they were brilliant mathematicians didn't hurt either. In my opinion, their method was not by any means gambling. Why? Yes, they were placing a wager on an uncertain event, but if they kept applying the same rules over enough hands, the result would not be uncertain. This is very similar to trading in that you can lose on some trades, but what does the picture look like after 100 trades? If a good trading methodology is used, it should be profitable over a 100-trade sample.

Another movie that makes this clear is *Rounders*. The question asked at the end of the movie is "Why do the same people keep winning the World Series of Poker?" Poker is referred to as advantage gambling; the term seems like an oxymoron. Doesn't the house always have the advantage? Not if you are playing poker. If you have enough skill, it is possible to have an advantage over the other players at the table. Trading is similar in that if you apply your sharply honed skills, you can have an advantage. Conversely, if you are lazy and don't have enough skill, you are guaranteed to fail.

One Commodity Trading Advisor (CTA) I used to work with said that a good trading system is—get ready for this—boring! Yes, trading for the most part is boring. If you need adrenaline in your life, don't find it trading financial instruments. Skydive, bungee jump, or engage in some other extreme sport if you need "action." If you are looking for "action" with trading, you instantly put yourself at a disadvantage when trading against professionals. To illustrate, I met a student of mine in Las Vegas who put himself through college by playing poker. He said the best time to play was on the weekends because there are more people visiting Las Vegas on the weekend than on the weekdays; they come to have a good time, drink, and gamble.

Further, he said that during the week you will see most of the local professionals playing in the casinos, and you can tell just by looking at a table whether the players are professionals. Everyone is drinking water, no one is laughing, and they all have a very large stack of chips in front of them. He added that it's possible to win in that situation, but it's much harder than playing against the unsuspecting tourists on the weekend. They fly in, laugh, drink, get distracted, give their money away, and call it "just having some fun." You get the point. If your aim is to "have some fun" trading, expect to make a large donation to the professionals of Wall Street.

SETTING REALISTIC EXPECTATIONS

H.M. Gartley, in his 1935 classic *Profits in the Stock Market*, states, "This course, concerning the technical approach to the business of trading stocks, is not to be considered as the philosopher's stone of the stock market." As you may or may not know, Gartley's use of the term "philosopher's stone" represented the archaic alchemist's goal of turning base metals into gold. The promises of Wall Street are no different today. "Turn $10,000 into $1,000,000!" is the cry of many promoters and brokers. Ask yourself, how many alchemists have been successful turning lead into gold?

In the forecourt of the temple of Apollo at Delphi was the inscription "Know Thyself." The idea behind this statement is that once you know yourself, or become self aware, only then will you really be able to understand other people. This is an important concept for the trader, because one of the most difficult aspects of trading is to identify the style of trading that suits your personality the best. Personally, when I started trading, I thought I was a real risk taker or "gunslinger." After losing some of my hard-earned cash, I quickly realized how risk averse I really was. Unfortunately, many of us have to learn the hard way and lose lots of money before we determine what our particular level of risk tolerance really is.

The French have a saying, "You don't even know what you want." When it comes to trading, how do you define success? How much profit do you expect to make trading? These questions must be answered specifically. We can't define trading success by saying "I want to make money." If your description of trading success is simply that you want to make money, then go buy a T-bill at Wells Fargo that pays out 2 percent a year and call yourself a successful T-bill trader. My personal goals of trading success are (1) positive monthly rates of return and (2) double-digit annual rate of return year after year. Every person must identify his or her own definition of success in regard to trading, and it will be different for everyone. If you were Bill Gates, then maybe buying T-bills at Wells Fargo is not such a bad idea; one billion at 2 percent is 20 million dollars per year. Could you live on that?

Unfortunately, most of us don't have a billion or so kicking around, so we might have to try to increase our rate of return by more than 2 percent. Some people might scoff at a 2 percent return; however these same people have probably generated a −1,000 percent return in their trading accounts during the past month. The point is to be realistic. There will always be someone telling you that you can obtain a triple digit-return, year after year forever (or less than triple digits in Madoff's case). Look at the returns of the top traders of the world, traders that manage funds with hundreds of millions of dollars. Is there a single trader out there that has been able to generate a triple-digit return, year after year for 10 years? No. So keep it real—double digits. I remember one CTA saying that if you can generate a 20 percent annual rate of return with a minimal drawdown (peak-to-valley dip in your equity curve), you will have almost unlimited money thrown at you to trade with. In *Profits in the Stock Market*, Gartley stated

> As in any human activity, the stock market student will find that, as he progresses in a systematic study of the market, the usual cloud of bewilderment will disappear. It is to be clearly understood as a primary premise in making this study, that neither the author nor any other writer is able to hand the reader a foolproof, automatic, and perfect system of beating the stock market. In the opinion of this writer, it is unlikely that there will ever come a time when an individual or group of individuals, even by elaborate and careful studies, will be able to call every turn in the market in advance. The reader should not object to this. The primary object of this course is to teach the average man to know enough about stock price movements so that he may consistently make a substantial profit every year. A reasonable objective of the average man would be to make 18–24 percent or more on the capital employed without the use of borrowed money.

Sorry to break it to you, but remember, as my Buddhist friend said, "Don't expect anything, and you will always be happy!"

DEBUNKING UNREALISTIC EXPECTATIONS

When I decided to get involved in the business of trading, I thought one of the best ways to learn would be to get licensed as a broker for futures. That didn't seem to help me much, so then I obtained my equities license. Still feeling that something was missing, I obtained my options license. I quickly found out that the mainstream licensing courses for stocks/commodities/options in the United States *and* Canada are sadly remiss in providing any practical trading strategies. If the official government-sanctioned license materials don't teach you practical trade strategies, then where should you turn? Should you attend that free trading seminar at the Sheraton this weekend?

As I'm sure you are aware, the investment education business is full of snake-oil salesman. Who should you listen to? Someone who says you *might* make 25 percent in a year, or someone who tells you that you will *certainly* make 100 percent in the next month? There really is a sucker born every minute; otherwise. the swindlers would be out of business. That is why there is always an infomercial on at 2 A.M. promising untold riches, with all those average couples making buckets of money every time they do a trade. Ask yourself, is it really education, or is it an attempt to sell you a course or a piece of software? Do your due diligence and look up the company on the Internet. Talk to current and former students. It's amazing how many people drop $10,000 for a course based on a good pitch. Remember, you can't buy success. The ads are compelling aren't they? They promise a 100 percent annual rate of return. It's hard not to fantasize; "if I put in $10,000 and I double it every year for 10 years I will have over 100 million in 10 years!" I consider these ads financial pornography.

Pick up a copy of *Technical Analysis of Stocks and Commodities* and you will see literally hundreds of trading systems for sale. I'm not saying that all systems are bad, but unfortunately some of the guerrilla marketing tactics are extreme. I remember one ad in which the vendor showed that his mom was trading his system and making oodles of money. It turned out that the CFTC (Commodity Futures Trading Commision) found out she wasn't trading the system. Needless to say, this vendor went out of business after receiving a hefty fine.

What about the expensive trading systems? Maybe they are better than the cheap ones; you get what you pay for—right? Not always. I met a system vendor at a trade show who was promoting his latest trading system. The vendor had an incredible booth, big screens, enthusiastic sales people, amazing brochures. I remarked to him, "I can't believe that your system is $20,000 when the other ones here are a few hundred or a few thousand dollars." His reply? "Instant credibility!" Now he's out of business as well.

Some of these organizations start to look similar to a cult in the sense that there is always an omniscient "guru." This demigod appears to have some miraculous ability to call every market turn. This amazing skill can be passed on to select initiates for a price. Asking questions like "Where are your brokerage statements or track record?" is like asking, "Where does a circle begin?" Some are swindlers that lost their stock or futures licenses because of an SEC or NFA (National Futures Association) ruling and are now self-proclaimed "experts" in regard to investment education. They sell the dream of instant success. If it was that easy, why aren't they just trading for themselves or managing money for other people? The hucksters will always tell you that making money trading is easy. Yes it is true, trading can be easy. But winning a lottery can be "easy" too, if you have the winning ticket.

CAN YOU SIT?

In my opinion, most speculators that trade derivatives have a common trait—lack of patience. To be a professional trader, they believe, requires having a real-time data feed, a lightning-fast Internet connection, and intraday charts. They feel that this technology gives them their much needed "trading edge" over their low-tech counterparts. Unfortunately, the opposite is more likely. Most impatient traders can't wait for days or weeks to execute their trades and feel they must execute orders off of intraday data perhaps several times a day. This behavior becomes even more important if a spouse is monitoring their time spent in front of the computer "trading." The professional trader knows that trading is not necessarily about the quantity of transactions one executes in one day. Patience is required if one is to wait for an ideal Gartley Pattern. The anxious, impatient trader typically doesn't want to wait for ideal setups and will often see "trading mirages." If you are a contrarian, then you will see the wisdom in trading off of the charts that the rookies avoid. When it comes to trading, we have to do the exact opposite of what the retail traders are doing. We know that most of them are losing money. So what we have to do is quite simple: find out what they are doing and do the exact opposite. This is hard, as we have all been programmed with the "conventional trading wisdom."

Regarding patience and waiting for ideal trade setups, I quote one of the greatest traders of all time, Jesse Livermore, who said in his classic book *Reminiscences of a Stock Operator*,

> And right here let me say one thing: After spending many years in Wall Street and after making and losing millions of dollars I want to tell you this: It never was my thinking that made the big money for me. It always was my sitting. Got that? My sitting tight! It is no trick at all to be right on the market. You always find lots of early bulls in bull markets and early bears in bear markets. I've known many men who were right at exactly the right time, and began buying and selling stocks when prices were at the very level which should show the greatest profit. And their experience invariably matched mine—that is, they made no real money out of it. Men who can both be right and sit tight are uncommon. I found it one of the hardest things to learn. But it is only after a stock operator has firmly grasped this that he can make big money. It is literally true that millions come easier to a trader after he knows how to trade than hundreds did in the days of his ignorance.

Livermore talks about making money *sitting*. Take note of the lesson here. In view of the foregoing, it appears that unless you are a professional market maker with inside information or an arbitrage trader, you should listen to Livermore and be patient and sit.

MORE TRANSACTIONS = LESS PROFIT

There is definitely a relationship between trading profits and the time frame in which we trade. Shorter time frames usually mean more transactions in a day versus fewer transactions generated by someone trading off of a daily chart. The cost of these transactions can be substantial. The new trader may conclude that fees and commissions of $10 per transaction amount to nothing compared to the vast sums he will make trading. If that same trader did five trades in a month, he would spend $50 per month. However if the same trader decides to trade intraday and does five trades per day, his costs would be $1,000 per month! Imagine starting every month $1,000 in the hole; it's a chore every month just to break even!

The promoters of intraday trading, such as broker/dealers or their agents, are the ones who stand to benefit the most from the quantity of your transactions. Win, lose, or draw, they will always make money on your transactions. If someone is encouraging you to trade intraday, ask the question, "Why?" I know of one trader who was trying to do some hedging a few years ago with a Forex dealer in Switzerland. He bought a contract, sat on the position for 60 days, and didn't execute any other trades. He received his statement in the mail thereafter informing him that they liquidated his position and closed his account! Obviously, they weren't interested in someone who was going to trade a few times per year.

Many broker/dealers view themselves as croupiers that are employed to facilitate what they believe is your inevitable demise. Some condescendingly look down on the retail trading public, viewing them as having terminal cancer, and consider themselves as simply "making them feel comfortable while they are still with us." I would like to think that this attitude doesn't exist, but it does. It's easy to start thinking like that when *everyone* in your brokerage office does. I almost fell into that way of thinking over 10 years ago. I refused to accept that "everyone eventually loses." Don't get me wrong, there are lots of ethical broker/dealers out there, and it's hard to choose one when you can't meet face to face. So make sure you get referrals from other happy clients. Broker/dealers are a necessary intermediary to allow us access to the financial markets. The good news is that with the advent of electronic trading as opposed to open outcry, the costs have come down significantly during the past decade. This enables the "little guy" to have a fighting chance to make money by keeping transaction costs low.

I'M A TRADER

When I was a naïve young speculator, I remember I opened my first futures account in the 1990s. I was so proud of myself; it sounded so good—"I'm a futures trader." Wow! I was actually surprised to find out how few people actually knew what that meant. However, the general apathy of the public didn't stop me from boasting about my new career to all who would listen. An accountant friend of mine from Canada named Brad was one of the few to whom I preached who knew what a futures trader was and what it involved. He congratulated me and gave me an analogy that I have never forgotten.

As you may know, Canadians love hockey, and so Brad used an illustration that included Canada's favorite sport. He said that you can buy all the hockey pads, helmets, skates, and sticks, but that doesn't make you an NHL professional. Even if you were invited to play a professional game with the Vancouver Canucks, does it mean that you will score a goal and lead the team to victory? He reminded me that the players are very good at what they do and are compensated accordingly: they are professionals. Without exception, they have all practiced most of their lives to get to where they are. They didn't attend a "Learn how to be an NHL professional in one weekend" seminar. Just good old blood, sweat, and tears from childhood got them to where they are.

It can be easy to play hockey, but will you score the goals to win the game? Imagine you have all the gear, you are playing in a real televised NHL game, and now you have the puck. You think, "Wow, if I can get this puck in that goal, I'll be a star." You look up and notice that the opposing team members are skating over to your vicinity in a very aggressive manner. You could rationalize, "Maybe they are coming over to ask me to be on their team because I'm so good at this!" or "Maybe these guys are lonely and want me to be their friend." Not! They are coming to take the puck away from you and put it in your goal, and it's not going to be pretty. Brad's illustration is a good one for new traders. When you open an account, it's like buying the equipment; when you fund your account, you are in the game. When you have a position on, you have the puck and the professionals are skating toward you to take the puck (money) away from you.

DO I NEED A COMPUTER?

I am of the opinion that with the advent of the Internet, cheap computers, and $300 Forex accounts, there are more bad traders now than ever before in human history. Unfortunately, some traders feel that trading can't be done without a computer. You might be intimidated by the processing power, storage, and so forth of these machines in comparison to our seemingly limited minds. You may rely on a machine to such an extent that you can't make a trading decision without it. By the end of this book, I will empower you with techniques that will allow you to make a trading decision and to trade *without* a computer.

Before personal computers, did anyone trade? Of course! And some of these seeming low-tech individuals made substantial sums of money without a computer. Market legends like W.D. Gann and H.M. Gartley did not hide behind technology or buy a magic piece of trading software. They did the unthinkable—they used their minds. The human mind is still the most complicated organism in the known universe. Let's get back to basics and start using it.

Computers, in regard to trading, should never be viewed as a replacement for the human mind, but rather as a convenience tool to speed up our analysis of the markets. To illustrate, imagine that you wanted to start framing houses for a living. To get started, you could "cheap out" and not buy any tools to start your business. You could go out on the street and pick up a large stone to use as a replacement for a hammer. There is no doubt that you really could frame a house with some nails and a stone. However, wouldn't it make sense to buy a hammer—or even better, a nail gun? Imagine all the time you could save. So it is with traders and computers. The computer will save you a lot of time when it comes to your analysis of the markets. However, you should still be able to frame a house with a rock, and you should still be able to trade without a computer. If you are a great trader, you should be able to use the same tools that the traders of yesteryear used: pencil, eraser, graph paper, slide rule (okay, calculator).

I remember conducting a Forex trading seminar in Chicago a few years ago when I noticed one of the students walking around the room showing the other students some pictures. Thinking that he was showing off his new girlfriend or his dog or his boat, I walked up and asked to have a look. He showed me a picture of his trading room with four monitors. I asked what he was showing these pictures for. He said that he wanted to show everyone that he was serious about trading. (I later found out that this "serious trader" never had a real account and had been paper trading for the past five years.) Lesson? Technology does not a great trader make.

We've all heard the computer geek's axiom, "garbage in, garbage out." Computer hardware is meaningless unless it is running a piece of software. So using a computer to help you make a trading decision is really software dependent. And software is, as we know, fallible, as are humans. There is no silver bullet when it comes to software.

I believe that most system traders fail when they remove the human element from the trading decision process. Is it really possible to program all potential future events that could affect the financial markets into a piece of software? No. If you want to try to do that, you will die trying as a programmer, not as a trader. Yes, computers can be intimidating; however, do not underestimate the power of the human mind.

To illustrate the superiority of the human mind over machines, I met a rocket scientist from Silicon Valley at a speaking engagement. He said that he worked on the computers for the space shuttle. He told me that there are five redundant computers on the space shuttle that are able to land it without human interaction. If the first computer fails, the next one kicks in; if that one fails, the next one kicks in, and so on. He then asked me how many times I thought the space shuttle landed via the computers. I answered, "Every time!?" He replied, "Never." As you could probably guess, I was astounded. The astronauts in the space shuttle are convinced that they are better at landing the shuttle than a computer. And by the way, do you think that NASA buys refurbished DOS laptops from garage sales? Does NASA hire high school dropouts at minimum wage to write computer code for them? No; they have the best hardware available and the brightest minds in the world writing software for these computers.

Despite the advanced technology, the astronauts on the space shuttle believe in the superiority of the human mind in regard to landing a space craft on the Earth. Likewise, professional traders believe in the superiority of the human mind when it comes to the less complicated aspect of trading financial instruments. To prove my point further, the rocket scientist said that when they ran simulations on the five different computers to land the space shuttle, each of the five computers landed the space shuttle differently, despite the fact that the computers are all exact duplicates of each other!

In the financial arena, the future is all about probabilities, not certainties. Mankind has free will, and there is no way for a human being to determine the actions of a single person in the future with 100 percent accuracy. However, there is a tendency for people to behave in a certain way under certain circumstances. When these circumstances present themselves, we can take advantage of the fact that the odds are temporarily in our favor.

CHAPTER 2

Technical Analysis 101

A hard fact for many analytical personality types to accept is that technical analysis is more of an art than a science. Gartley describes the technical approach, again in *Profits in the Stock Market,* as follows:

> Briefly defined, the technical approach is a study of recurring phenomena which appear in the price trend as a result of the supply and demand relation of the shares traded on the stock exchanges. Essentially, it is a study of the effects which fundamental changes cause in the price trends of shares.

I agree with this definition and define technical analysis in this book as using historical price data to determine future price action. A "pure" technician does not include fundamental data in his analysis; he assumes that the market has already digested this information so that it is already reflected in the price. We will present some basic information in this chapter, covering only the technical methods that are needed to identify Gartley Patterns, while avoiding the methods used by the more than 90 percent of the trading population that loses money.

FUNDAMENTALS VERSUS TECHNICALS

People often ask, "How do you trade—do you use fundamentals or technicals"? Most retail traders often say they like technical trading, because they believe that it is easier to trade pure technicals than trying to interpret the fundamentals. This is a valid point. As

Gartley mentioned regarding technical analysis, "it is a study of the effects which fundamental changes cause." In view of this statement, we come to the conclusion that fundamentals primarily drive the markets, not the technicals. Then why use technicals at all?

Technical analysis works best in the absence of fundamental shocks to the market. *Most of the time*, there are no fundamental shocks to the specific market that we are trading. However, there are times when scheduled or unscheduled news events take place. If the news is a surprise and the information has not already been digested by the market, there will be a strong directional move to compensate for this new fundamental information. At this moment in time, the price of the instrument you are trading has to "reset" itself based on this new information. Typically, the increased volatility and sudden price action slows down within 30 minutes. During this "reset" time, all technical analysis should be disregarded, inasmuch as it is the fundamental shock that is driving the price. After this brief period has elapsed, then technical analysis starts to govern the instrument once again.

Why does technical analysis work? The human mind has a desire to create order. You are created in God's image, and God is a God of order, not disorder. When you see a mess, you want the mess to be cleaned up and organized. This is true in regard to your home, yards, vehicles, and the like, because you prefer order to disorder. This concept also applies to the financial markets. When you look at a chart, the first thing that you see is chaos, and it is your instinct to create order out of chaos in accord with the Freemasons' Latin motto, Ordo ab Chao. You examine the chart carefully to make some sort of sense (order) of it. Depending on the programming that your brain has received, you might start to see things based on your acquired technical knowledge. However, it is your instinct, whether it is conscious or not, to look for geometric shapes. If you don't agree, look around you at the shape of this book, the shape of your house, room, car, and property; humans prefer order and geometry. You prefer circles, squares, triangles, and proportion.

This tendency is also reflected in your interpretation of trading charts. This is the primary reason that technical analysis works. There is a tendency for humans to behave in a certain way based on the geometric shapes that appear on a price chart. All patterns that develop on a chart can be identified with the shapes of the circle, the square, and the triangle. Later, we will discuss how the Gartley Pattern relates to geometric shapes and other classical technical patterns. When humans identify these shapes on the conscious or subconscious level, they will behave in a predictable manner. This allows us to make a prediction of what will happen in the future.

SHOULD YOU PREDICT THE FUTURE?

Some of us might not consciously think about it, but maybe we have been brought up with the idea that "predicting the future" is wrong. Maybe you have read in the Torah that practitioners of divination are condemned by God. If so, you probably have a conflict within yourself about the issue of predicting the future. If you have felt this way, you are not alone; I felt this conflict for a number of years. However, consider this real-life experience that helped me keep things in perspective.

I was staying at a hotel in Santa Clara, California preparing to speak about trading currencies. It was 8 A.M. and I was scheduled to speak at 9 A.M. I just woke up, my clothes were still in my suitcase from traveling, I hadn't showered in over 24 hours, and I was starving. On the dresser in my hotel room was a coupon for a free breakfast buffet in the lobby, and the expiration time on the coupon was 10 A.M. Get out your crystal ball and predict what happened. Yes, you are correct. I jumped in the shower, ironed my clothes, ate the free breakfast, and started speaking at exactly 9 A.M. Did you have to compromise your principles or worship the devil to make this prediction? Of course not. I firmly believe that every human being has free will and that we are not predestined. Despite your guess as to what I would do between 8 A.M. and 9 A.M. in the hotel that day, I could have slept in, put on wrinkly clothes, and started the seminar late, hungry, and stinky. It was possible, but not probable.

Trading is based on probabilities, not certainties. There is definitely a certain way that markets will behave under normal circumstances. But there are always exceptions to the rule. So making a prediction about the future with trading is simply trying to determine what the collective person (the market) will do in the next minute, day, week, or month; it doesn't have to do with divination. (However, some still try to use divination. I know of a broker who had a "witchdoctor" try to help his client with an underwater cattle position. It didn't help!)

SETTING UP CHARTS

With so many chart types, some traders don't know where to start. Should I use open, high, low, close (OHLC) bar charts? Japanese candlestick charts? Point and figure charts? The list goes on and on. Which one is best? It really depends on which technical methods you will be using. If your trade strategies don't consider opening and closing prices, is there any need to use candlestick charts? As we will be looking for patterns, emphasis will naturally be placed on the extreme highs and lows of the price action versus the opening and closing prices. Therefore the good old open, high, low, close bar chart will suit our purposes just fine.

As discussed, the need to create order out of disorder is human nature. Another human instinct that applies to trading is a desire to divide things evenly. When you see a hot pizza come out of a wood-fired oven, what do you want to do? Cut it in half, then quarters, then eighths. The desire to divide also applies to the price axis and the time axis of our price charts. In regard to time, we like to divide one day, 24 hours or

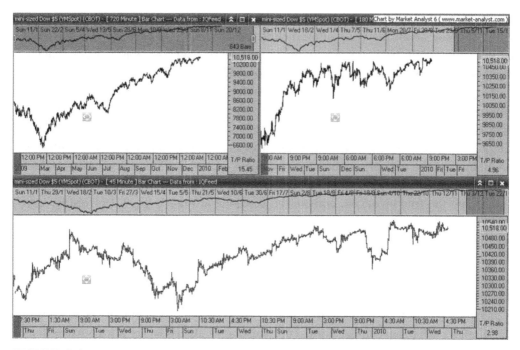

FIGURE 2.1 Workbook with 720-,180-, and 45-Minute Charts

1440 minutes in half or 12 hours or 720 minutes. We now divide 12 hours into 6 hours or 360 minutes. Half of 6 hours is 3 hours or 180 minutes. Half of 180 is 90 minutes and half of 90 is 45 minutes. These are the natural divisions of a 24 hour period. Don't keep all these charts, as you can find patterns over these different time frames with a minimum of three charts. In Figure 2.1, I have saved 720-, 180-, and 45-minute charts of the mini-sized Dow. This page is located within a Workbook that has been created, entitled Indices.

Most software packages allow you to save a Workspace or Workbook. Each Workbook will allow you to save a page. Each page allows you to save a chart or charts. In addition to the page displayed, other pages are saved within the Indices Workbook such as the E-mini S&P and Nasdaq. Create additional Workbooks in a similar manner with titles such as Agricultural Products, Metals, Softs, Energies, and U.S. Equities.

Since there is a relationship between the x and y axes (price and time) on our charts, we need to allocate space on our charts to account for time on the weekends. Therefore if your software allows you to display calendar days instead of trading days, turn this function on. The software will display a space between the Friday and Monday trading sessions to show time passing on the weekend. An example of a calendar day chart appears in Figure 2.2.

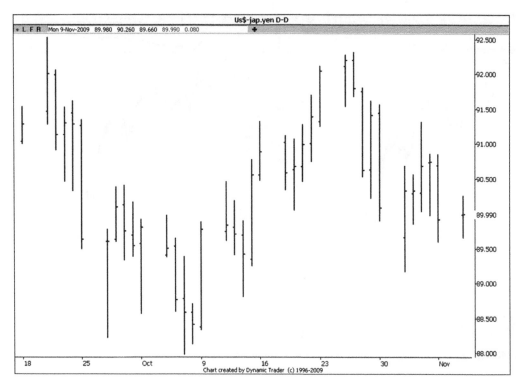

FIGURE 2.2 Calendar Day Chart

It is important to note that trading takes place on the weekend, but not on a physical exchange; it happens in the trader's mind. When the trader is spending time on the weekend doing other activities, he is still thinking about trading and making decisions that he will carry out on Monday when the market opens. This is why there is usually increased volume and volatility on Mondays as the market catches up to the "weekend trading."

The most common method of displaying price data on a chart is the arithmetic scale. The vertical *y* or price axis of the chart with arithmetic scaling will display equidistant price levels. For example, if the vertical distance on the chart between $10 and $20 is one inch, the vertical distance between $20 and $30 is one inch. For the purposes of this book, we will be using arithmetic scaling. Gartley discusses the value of logarithmic and square-root scaling, and there is value in using a logarithmic scale when discovering Gartley Patterns on larger time frames. However, we will leave it up to the readers' discretion as to how much time they wish to devote to the study of logarithmic and square-root scaling. Figure 2.3 displays a chart of the DJI (Dow Jones Industrials) index over 1.5 years. The left chart is an arithmetic scale chart, and the right chart is a logarithmic chart. Notice the prices of each chart in the middle of the screen.

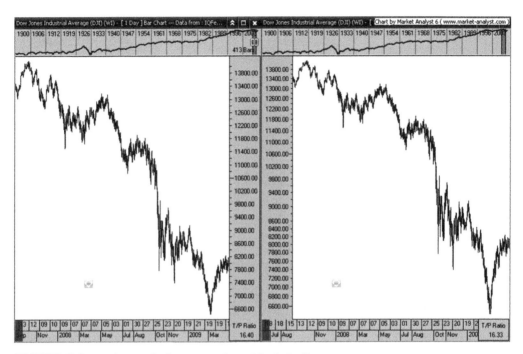

FIGURE 2.3 Arithmetic Scaling versus Logarithmic Scaling

SWING CHARTS

One of the more difficult aspects of pattern recognition in the financial markets is determining where each swing begins and ends. Patterns seem easy to identify after the fact, but the key to successful trading is finding a potential pattern before it is complete. One way to filter through all the "noise" and find important highs and lows is through the use of swing charts. In the world of technical analysis, there are many ways to construct a swing chart; for the purposes of our discussion, we will construct a swing chart based on price and time. Many technical analysis software packages include a zigzag indicator. This indicator will draw a line between each of the significant highs and lows. There are never two highs or lows plotted in a row; it is always alternating high, low, high, low, and so on. How does the software calculate when to draw a new line between a new high or low? The zigzag indicator will usually have a sensitivity setting. A highly sensitive zigzag indicator will plot many zigzag lines, and a less sensitive setting will plot fewer lines. The sensitivity setting of the zigzag indicator focuses on the change in price by a variable percentage. The chart in Figure 2.4 displays a percent swing chart overlay.

For example, let's imagine we plot a zigzag indicator on a chart of the EUR/USD and the sensitivity is set to 1 percent. The EUR/USD has rallied from 1.4000 to 1.4500 without a retracement of more that 1 percent (140–145 points). In this case, the zigzag

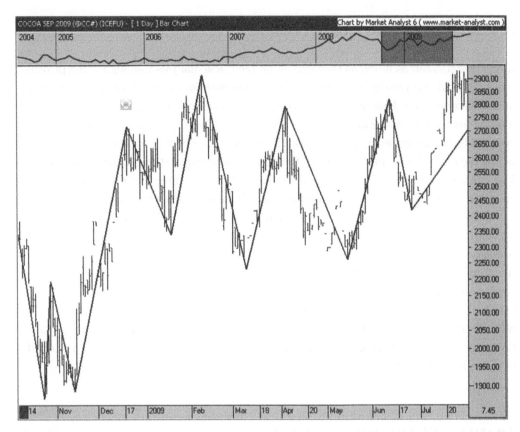

FIGURE 2.4   Percent Swing Chart Overlay

indicator will plot a line between the low at 1.4000 and the high at 1.4500. Now there is a decline of 100 points in the EUR/USD from 1.4500 high down to 1.4400. The previous line in the zigzag indicator will still be displayed from the low of 1.4000 to the 1.4500 high, and a new line will not be displayed from the 1.4500 high to the 1.4400 low. Why is this? When the sensitivity is set to 1 percent, you are telling the software to show you new lines only when there is a one percent change in price. The assumption is that unless there is a one percent change in price in the opposite direction, the current bullish trend is still in effect. Therefore in the foregoing example, we believe that the trend at this point is still up, because the market has not reversed by at least 1 percent in the opposite direction. A new line would be plotted only if the EUR/USD moves down from 1.4500 to 1.4355 (1.4500 − .145). This example allows us to construct a swing chart based on price only. Time is also an important concept that must be accounted for in regard to swing charts. If the software you use has a minimum amount of time or bars to be counted as a new swing, even better; otherwise, your swing chart analysis could be thrown off by an outlier.

OSCILLATORS AND INDICATORS

Retail traders read as much as they can about technical analysis looking for the prover-bial holy grail. Eventually, we learn about the hundreds of lagging technical indicators and oscillators. Like kids in a candy store, we test each one on each different market, looking for the one that will allow us to retire early. It is very convenient to have these colorful lines automatically plotted directly on the price chart or in a separate window below the chart. This type of technical tool is very appealing to the general "lazy" public. You can apply the indicator to the chart once, and the indicator line updates automati-cally with each new bar added without any additional input from the user.

Eventually the newbie realizes that there is "no free lunch" when it comes to trad-ing with these indicators and that they aren't magic. Most of the popular indicators and oscillators are simply taking the price data from the chart and displaying it in an alterna-tive form (one of the exceptions is volume; see the following discussion). Though these squiggly lines are called different names, they are all really doing the same thing; they are simply reflecting the current price action on the chart. They are not providing any new information. To make matters worse, the more indicators that you apply to your chart, the more duplication you have of the same information. What we need to do is to add new, leading information.

TRADING IN THE WHITE SPACE

Lagging indicators are only as good as the last bar of data displayed on the chart; typ-ically, they don't extend past the last bar of price data. Conversely, there are technical drawing tools available that provide information that extends past the last bar of data. An example of this is a trendline. A trendline uses current and previous price action to project a line off into the future past the last bar of data on the chart. Many charts will display the last bar of data right up against the price axis without any "white space" be-tween the price axis and the last bar of data. If possible, change the settings on your software to display some white space so as to view the future projections of your leading indicators. Now that we have made some white space to work with between the price axis and the last bar of price data, we can use some leading indicators to make an edu-cated guess as to what might happen in the future. The white space is the canvas of the technician. We are now able to paint a picture of what we think the future might look like. Figure 2.5 displays an example of how the stochastic oscillator ends abruptly at the last bar of data, while the Fibonacci retracement and the trendline extend off into the white space.

FIGURE 2.5 Limitations of Oscillators and Indicators

VOLUME

Unlike the oscillators previously described that simply massage and reinterpret price data that is already on the price chart, volume provides a different dimension to our technical method of trading. As is shown later on, we will use volume analysis as one of the "rules" to find a valid Gartley Pattern. Most traders that trade Gartley Patterns today do not include volume as part of their criteria.

In *Profits in the Stock Market*, Gartley discusses the use of volume analysis extensively. He says, in part,

> Theoretically, the reason we study volume is because it is believed that it is a measure of supply of and demand for shares. . . . Every price change occurs as the result of a transaction consisting of the sale and purchase of shares of stock. The number of shares involved in such a transaction constitutes volume. Every transaction is the result of the meeting of demand, on the one hand, with supply on the other. When demand exceeds supply, prices tend to rise. Conversely when supply exceeds demand, prices tend to fall.

Summarizing his discussion on volume, Gartley defines specific rules for us in regard to volume as follows:

After a long decline has taken place, and the trend begins to rise, an increase of volume on minor rallies, and a decrease on a minor declines, is of important bullish significance. Conversely, after an extended advance, a decrease of column on minor rallies, and an increase on minor declines is of important bearish significance. As a general rule, volume decreases during a bear market, and increases during a bull market. The peaks of volume in bull markets appear just preceding the intermediate tops, near the end of major phases. The highest points of volume are seldom exactly the top levels. During a corrective phase of a bull market, one of the characteristics in judging their termination is a steady decrease in volume, with volume at a low level as the correction reaches its end, just before the resumption of the major up-trend. In bear markets, selling climaxes are accompanied by a sharp increase in volume, as panic reaches its peak. During rallies in bear markets (corrective phases), volume shows a tendency to decrease from the high level of the selling climax, but will frequently rise at the top of the corrective phase.

Gartley's volume guidelines are revisited in Part Two of this book. An example of volume plotted on a price chart can be seen in Figure 2.6.

An aspect of technical trading that we should be wary of is the occurrence of periods of low volume. Many exchange-traded products are trading 24/5 (my prediction is that it will eventually be 24/7, like Vegas). However, most of these products will experience lower than normal volume at some point during a 24-hour period. Remember, technical analysis works best in the absence of fundamental shocks to the market and when there is volume.

DATA SOURCES

Google "financial market data" and see how many hits you get. There are many financial data vendors anxious to get you to subscribe to their feed for a small monthly fee. This real-time or end-of-day (EOD) data can be read by a standalone charting package or used with a "free" charting package provided by the data vendor. As technical traders, we must have access to the most accurate data to identify Gartley Pattern trade signals. Do not be cheap when it comes to market data. Do your due diligence and choose a tier-one data vendor with clean, quality data from the various exchanges that you wish to trade.

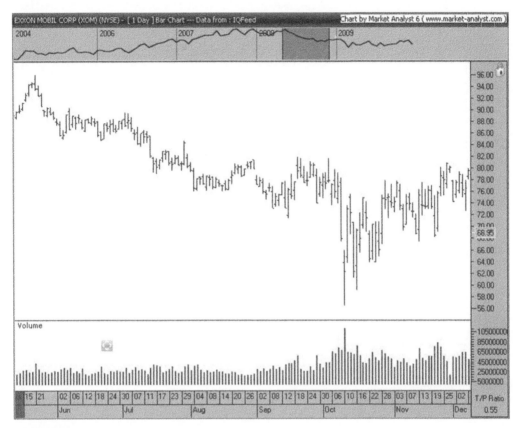

FIGURE 2.6 Volume

Regarding futures contracts, try to use spot or cash data for your charts. If these are not available, use continuous contracts that roll at contract expiration or are based on volume. A continuous chart is created by chaining front-month futures contracts together. When a contract expires, the next bar of data displayed is based on the next contract that is closest to expiration (the "front month"). By creating a continuous contract in this manner, we can view a chart over a number of months or years.

CHAPTER 3

The Gartley and Elliott Wave Relationship

To fully appreciate the logic and unique market opportunities afforded to those that trade the Gartley Pattern, a brief description of Elliott Wave theory is necessary. If you know about Elliott Wave theory already, don't worry; I'm not going to spend too much time on it. In my opinion, as you will find out by the end of this book, one does not have to be an "Elliottician" to make money trading. If you like the sound of what we will be discussing in the next few pages, order *R.N. Elliott's Masterworks* to understand the details of the theory. However, I would prefer that you read about the Elliott Wave out of intellectual curiosity rather than looking for practical trade strategies. What we will discuss here briefly are the important parts of Elliott Wave theory so that you can have a better understanding of trends and counter trends.

If you don't know what the Elliott Wave is, here is the short version. In 1938, three years after H.M. Gartley published *Profits in the Stock Market*, R.N. Elliott wrote *The Wave Principle*. This publication, along with his final book, *Nature's Law—The Secret of the Universe*, introduced the trading world to the theory of a hidden order in the financial markets. In *The Wave Principle*, Elliott described a recurring cycle that comprises what he referred to as an impulsive phase (trend) followed by a corrective phase (counter trend). Elliott identified five legs or waves within each of the impulsive phases and three or more waves in the corrective phase (he stated that the three-leg correction was the most common). Elliott labeled each of the waves in the impulsive phase with a number (1, 2, 3, 4, 5) and each of the waves in the corrective phase with a letter (A, B, C). Impulsive and corrective phases can be either bullish or bearish. As can be seen in Figure 3.1, we are looking at a bullish five-wave sequence followed by a simple ABC zigzag correction. At the completion of this correction, a single eight-wave cycle is complete, and the expectation is that a new eight-wave cycle is about to begin.

FIGURE 3.1   Bullish Impulse and Correction Labeled

In our second example in Figure 3.2, we have a bearish five-wave sequence followed by a simple ABC zigzag correction. A percent swing chart overlay indicator has been applied to this example to make it easier to see the Elliott waves.

To further complicate things, Elliott stated that each of the waves within a 1, 2, 3, 4, 5, A, B, C cycle would subdivide into a smaller set of waves. The idea is that waves 1, 3 ,5, A, and C are in themselves impulsive phases whereas waves 2, 4, and B are in themselves corrective phases. Elliott claimed that there were waves within waves and that all of the waves are ordered according to what he referred to as degrees. As seen in Figure 3.3, Wave 1 (labeled as a 1 with a circle around it) is the beginning of a five-wave impulsive sequence of a particular degree. However, within this single wave there is a further subdivision of five waves of a lesser degree (labeled as 1, 2, 3, 4, and 5 with brackets). This in turn is followed by Wave 2, a corrective phase made up of a smaller three-wave correction. Figure 3.3 is a close-up shot of waves 1 and 2 from the bullish example shown in Figure 3.2.

Elliott described nine different degrees and how all markets conform to these natural laws. Elliott specified both inviolate rules and more flexible guidelines. Some of the Elliott Wave rules for a five-wave impulse are

1. Wave 2 should not exceed the beginning of Wave 1.

2. Wave 4 should not invade the territory of Wave 1.

3. Wave 3 is never the shortest.

FIGURE 3.2 Bearish Impulse and Correction Labeled

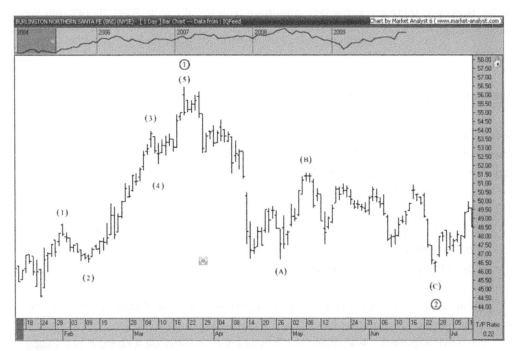

FIGURE 3.3 Elliott Subdivisions

If you find this confusing, don't worry; you don't need to know these details, given that the Gartley Trading Method replaces Elliott Wave. Those plagued with Elliott Wave obsessive compulsive disorder (EWOCD) believe that the Wave principle explains not just the financial markets but also the universe. This philosophical direction became evident when Elliott released his final book, entitled *Nature's Law—The Secret of the Universe*. I'm sorry to let you know (if you haven't found out already) that Elliott Wave theory does *not* reveal the secret of the universe. There is definitely a tendency for the market to behave in the fashion that Elliott described, but it is by no means a "natural law" like the law of gravity. Many who belong to the Elliott Wave cult believe that Elliott's system is pristine and perfect, and that if you aren't making money, it means you need to study it more deeply. I agree with William C. Garrett who wrote in his book *Investing for Profit with Torque Analysis of Stock Market Cycles*,

> In studying Elliott's patterns of movement, and trying to predict from the patterns, however, it soon became obvious that the patterns did not always fulfill their prospect. The rules were too rigid, and, by the time I was introduced to the theory, the rules had multiplied into a confusing array of exceptions.

Bottom line, if you want to read about Elliott Wave theory, read *The Wave Principle* written in 1938 by R.N. Elliott. Thereafter, I'm sure you will agree with William Garrett's comment; the theory has multiplied today into something more complicated than it used to be. However, there are some very important aspects of Elliott Wave theory that we must consider.

TRENDS AND COUNTER TRENDS

Ideally, all we are trying to do is to find the end of a counter trend to ride the trend. The hard part is to identify which phase we are in. The key takeaway from Elliott's theory is that there obvious structures that identify trend phases and counter-trend phases.

In *Profits in the Stock Market*, Gartley states,

> [W]e then must recognize that each intermediate cycle consists of two parts, namely a major phase which is the direction of the major or primary trend, and a corrective phase, counter to that trend.

Elliott's corrective phase can also be referred to as a counter-trend move. Following a trend (five-wave impulse phase) there is always a counter trend (corrective phase). The five-wave impulsive trend phase is always easy to identify on a chart; it is a strong

FIGURE 3.4 Trends and Counter Trends

directional move that does not have any overlapping waves. This impulsive phase is very different from a corrective phase that is made up of choppy market action with *overlapping* waves. It is imperative to understand which phase we are in so that we can identify valid Gartley Patterns at the completion of a counter-trend move. The cycle of a five-wave trend followed by the three-wave correction is shown in Figure 3.4.

In Figure 3.4 it appears that the trend is down and that a correction has just completed. We now assume that the existing bearish trend is going to reassert itself, because a bearish trend move (five-wave impulsive phase) usually follows the counter-trend move (typically an ABC corrective phase). What this means is that you will be trading in the direction of the trend, as indicated by the five-wave sequence, if you put on a trade at the end of the counter trend. This is a good thing, as we all know that it should be easier to make money trading an impulsive phase rather than a corrective one. Therefore, the ultimate trade setup would involve finding the end of a counter-trend move, and this is what the Gartley Trading Method accomplishes.

THE ALL-IMPORTANT CORRECTIVE PHASE

Elliott described so many different corrections in his book *The Wave Principle* that many Elliott traders have concluded that it's almost impossible to find the end of a corrective sequence. However, despite the fact that Elliott described so many corrections, he did say that one of those corrections is more common than all the others. Which correction was he referring to? Elliott referred to it as "the simple ABC zigzag correction." An important point to remember regarding this simple pattern is that the end of Wave C should always exceed the end of Wave A. The end of Wave C could be one of the most important levels that we can identify. Why? If the corrective phase is complete at the end of Wave C, that means that the market is about to enter an impulsive phase. If the simple ABC zigzag correction is the most common corrective sequence, then shouldn't it make sense to take note when a market has displayed one of these corrective structures and place a trade? Since the simple ABC zigzag correction is the most common, let's put the odds in our favor by taking a trade in the direction of the trend and trading all five waves of an impulsive phase. Remember, we are trying to trade with the trend, not against it, and we achieve this by getting in at the end of a corrective phase. As we will find out, this type of three-wave ABC structure is an important aspect of finding a valid Gartley Pattern.

When it comes to projecting the end of Wave C, the typical projection would be when the length of Wave C is equal to the length of Wave A. In other words, once we know the range of Wave A, we project that range from the end of Wave B to give us the typical projection for the end of Wave C. What technical drawing tool can we use to make a projection for the end of Wave C? We will be using the price-extension tool discussed later in this section to make end of wave C projections. Figure 3.5 provides an example of how we can use the price-extension tool when it is set to 100 percent to make an end of Wave C projection. Notice the symmetry between Wave A and Wave C?

AB = CD

The AB = CD label is used extensively in the trading community, and there is a relationship between AB = CD and the Elliott Wave ABC correction. In Figure 3.6 Gartley draws a bullish trendline between point A and point C. He then copies this line and plots it from point B. Notice that the angles of the two lines are identical and are parallel. As the market approaches point D, there is an expectation of a reversal because the AB leg is equivalent in price and time to the CD leg.

This type of AB = CD relationship between two waves moving in the same direction is also seen with other classical patterns, such as flag and pennant formations.

FIBONACCI RATIOS

It appears that the first person to start using the Fibonacci series of numbers in the financial markets was R.N. Elliott. Once again, we won't go into a great deal about this subject, but there is much more detailed information available in print and on the Web.

FIGURE 3.5 Wave A and Wave C Symmetry

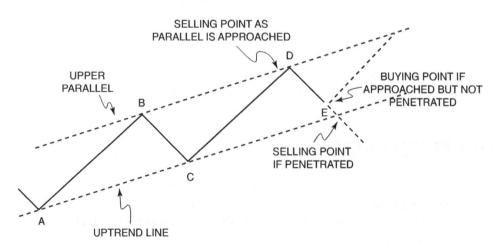

FIGURE 3.6 Bullish Trendline between Point A and Point C
Source: Gartley, H.M. *Profits in the Stock Market*, Lambert-Gann Publishing, 1935, page 249.

Leonardo of Pisa (c. 1170–c. 1250) or Fibonacci (son of Bonacci), was an Italian mathematician who convinced the Western world to drop Roman numerals and adopt the Hindu–Arabic numeral system. If you didn't know, there was resistance to this idea from the Church, because the Roman system started with the number one, which represented God. The Hindu–Arabic system had numbers before 1 (God) so this system didn't sit well with the Church. Especially the idea of zero, or as the church would interpret it, nirvana, a heretical concept not to be discussed by civilized medieval Christians. After arriving back in Pisa after traveling with his father in North Africa, Fibonacci wrote *Liber Abacci* (Book of the Abacus or the Book of Calculation) in 1202. In the third section of this book, he poses a problem: "How many pairs of rabbits can be produced in a year from one pair if each pair gives birth to a new pair each month starting with the second month?"

From this problem comes the number sequence that bears Leonardo's name to this day: 1, 1, 2, 3, 5, 8, 13, 21, 34, 55, 89, 144, and so on. Notice how any two adjacent numbers in the sequence add up to the next number in the sequence? As the numbers continue to infinity, the ratio between any number and the next higher number is approximately .618, and the ratio between any number and the next lower number is approximately 1.618. Interestingly enough, these numbers show up all over the place—in galaxies, flowers, music, DNA—and in the financial markets.

Other numbers can be derived from Fibonacci's sequence. The relationships between alternate numbers in the sequence are .382 and 2.618, and every third number gives us .236 and 4.235. Based on the foregoing information, we now have a series of numbers to be used for our trading applications: .236, .382, .618, 1, 1.618, 2.618, 4.235. However, many traders stop here and just use these numbers and miss out on the extra "secret" Fibonacci numbers. These are derived by obtaining the square root of the series previously listed. These "secret" numbers are .486, .786, 1.272, 2.058. Adding these numbers to the previous series gives us the following: .236, .382, .486, .618, .786, 1, 1.272, 1.618, 2.058, 2.618, 4.235, and so on.

This series was presented to the trading world in the early 1990s in Bryce Gilmore's classic book, *Geometry of the Markets II* (more on Bryce later).

PRICE RETRACEMENTS

A Fibonacci retracement tool or price-retracement tool can be found in most technical analysis software packages. Maybe you've looked at it, played with it, and never used it again. This tool and the price-extension tool are the two most important technical tools that we will be using to help us find valid Gartley Patterns.

To display Fibonacci retracements on a chart, the first thing we need to do is define the trend. In Figure 3.7, it appears that there is a downtrend that started in July and ended

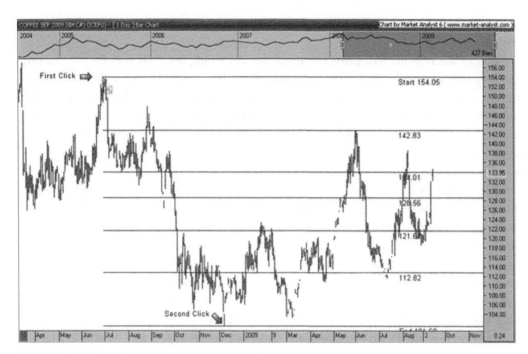

FIGURE 3.7 Price Retracements

in December. To display the horizontal Fibonacci retracement lines shown here, simply click where you think the trend begins and where you believe it ended. These points are displayed with the labels "First Click" and "Second Click." Now that the trend has been determined as bearish, you would be looking for selling opportunities, so that you trade in the direction of the trend. The Fibonacci retracement levels displayed show levels where there are potential resistance levels that provide an opportunity to sell short. The June high hit the 78.6 percent Fibonacci retracement almost to the tick.

The purpose of the price-retracement tool is to identify support or resistance at the end of a counter trend. The benefit of using price retracements is that we will never buy a high or sell a low. Referring again to this chart, it would have been possible to "wait for trend confirmation" and "wait for the market to tell us what direction it wants to go." Many traders would feel that a "conservative approach" would be to wait for the market to take out the December low and place sell orders below this point. What is the problem with this strategy? You could be doing the opposite of "buy low, sell high," and you could end up selling the low.

Notice the quotes in the preceding paragraph. These pithy sayings are part of the canon of the traditional Wall Street wisdom. Is it really "conservative" to sell the break below the December low if it is the low of the year? Have you ever done that? I have, and it's not fun. If you want to stop selling on a low, then stop. Remember the movie,

Network? Open your window now and scream, "I'm mad as hell, and I'm not going to take this anymore!"

One of the reasons that price retracements are so important is that they focus on two very important data points: the beginning of the trend and the end of the trend. The traders watching this trend have these two data points burned into their memory. We know that monuments are erected to honor soldiers in a war so that we "never forget." Similarly, at areas on a chart where there is a trend reversal, a significant battle has been fought. As they would treat a monument to honor the bulls and the bears that have died in battle, traders remember trend-reversal points.

Think of it this way; imagine that a stock promoter phones you to buy a penny stock. He says it's only 75 cents per share. You listen to him and buy some with the intention to possibly buy more. Shortly thereafter, the stock dips to a yearly low of 60 cents and then shoots straight up to 2.00 per share. What number would you think about? You would probably be thinking, like most people, "If only I had bought at 60 cents." Now the stock trades sideways between $2.00 and $2.10. You begin to wonder about selling it but you heard that it should go to $3.00 so you hold on to it. Suddenly it drops to $1.35 per share. What number are you thinking of now? "If only I had sold it at $2.10."

Can you see why these extreme highs and lows are so important? Now after these two price extremes have been made, most of the participants will do the following calculation: "If I had bought at 60 cents, then sold at $2.10, I could have made $1.50 per share." Look at the number $1.50. What number do you think of? Did you divide it in half to 75 cents? Without consciously thinking about it, you may be inclined, along with a lot of other traders of this stock, to call your broker and buy some more shares. Why? Because in the back of your mind you subtracted 75 cents from the high of $2.10 to arrive at the current price of the stock at $1.35. There has been a 50 percent retracement, and the stock now appears to have a 50 percent discount. As we will see, a 50 (48.6) percent retracement is a very important level of support or resistance.

The lines displayed in the retracement chart in Figure 3.7 are an example of internal price retracements. When most people discuss retracements, they are referring to internal retracements. It is possible to display additional lines on our charts that are referred to as external retracements. In the chart in Figure 3.7, any line that would extend beyond the 100 percent level at 154.05 would be an external retracement. We will concern ourselves with internal retracements only in our discussion of the Gartley Pattern.

PRICE EXTENSIONS

Many software packages provide this functionality under various titles, such as wave extension, Fibonacci projection, alternate price projection, and the like. These tools all

FIGURE 3.8 Using the Price Extension Tool to Calculate the End of Wave

perform a similar function. In this chapter, we refer to this technique as a price extension. To plot a price extension, one is required to input three data points. The first two data points are used to input the price range of the first leg, which we will refer to as Wave A. The third data point is used to determine where to project the range of Wave A from; this third data point will always be equivalent to the end of Wave B. An example is shown in Figure 3.8.

Notice that the range of Wave A (from point 1 to point 2) is equivalent to the range of Wave C (from point 3 to point 4).

Other technicians may use additional Fibonacci ratios when they use the price-extension tool; however, I continue to believe that the best number to be used with the price-extension tool is 100 percent.

Using Trendlines to Calculate Price Extensions

Some technical software packages don't include a price-extension tool to help us calculate the end of Wave C. If that is the case, don't despair; almost all charting packages

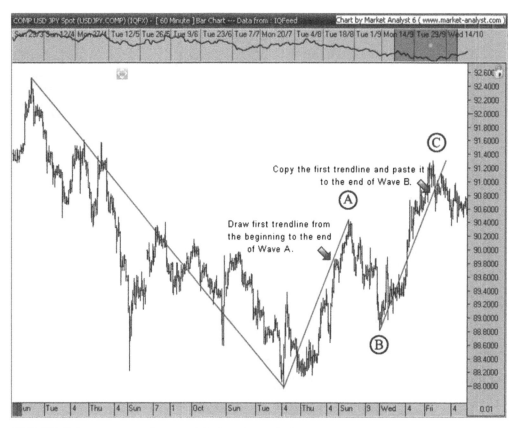

FIGURE 3.9 Using Trendlines to Calculate the End of Wave C

allow you to draw a trendline, and in this section we will consider how to use the lowly trendline to accomplish the same result as a price-extension tool.

Let's use Figure 3.9 as an example of how to use trendlines to calculate a price extension. The first step is to draw a trendline from the low at the beginning of Wave A to the high at the end of Wave A. Now copy the trendline that you have drawn. Next, paste the trendline to the low at the end of Wave B. As you can see, there are now two trendlines displayed on your chart. The first trendline is the measurement of the length and slope of Wave A, and the second is the estimate of the length and slope of Wave C. In fact, this technique of projecting the end of Wave C is superior to a price-extension tool in the sense that this routine includes a time projection. A price-extension tool displays only a horizontal line (price only), whereas the second trendline displayed to project the end of Wave C is a diagonal line (price *and* time). Therefore, the second trendline displayed shows us the end of the Wave C price projection at the price level where the second trendline terminates. In addition, the second trendline shows us the typical length of time that Wave C will take to complete, based on the length of Wave A.

FIGURE 3.10 Using a Quadrilateral to Calculate the End of Wave C

Using Quadrilaterals to Calculate Price Extensions

The final method that we will use to determine the end of Wave C is with the quadrilateral tool. Most software packages do not have this tool; if this is not available, use the trendline method described previously to make an end of Wave C projection.

To use the quadrilateral tool, first click the beginning of Wave A, then drag the quadrilateral until the side of it connects with the end of Wave B so that it looks like Figure 3.10.

THE BOTTOM LINE

At the conclusion of Part One, what have you learned? Be realistic, don't be greedy, and don't expect to make triple digits every month. Expect nothing, and you will always be happy. If you see an advertisement that seems too good to be true, then it is; I call it "financial pornography." Professional traders are able to make a trading decision and own it; they don't play the blame game. They are able to trade without a computer if they have to and are not enslaved to black box holy grail trading systems that they bought at a seminar. You have learned that patience is a virtue and that we sometimes need to "sit," as Livermore described it.

You have to know what kind of trader you are and what your risk tolerance is. You also have to define what "success" is in regard to trading. You can't define a successful trader as one who never suffers a loss. If so, then there are no successful traders in the world, because everyone at some point experiences a loss. In connection with this is the concept of "being right." Your worst enemy in this regard is an inflated ego—thus the need for humility. You learned that successful traders are not lazy and that this vocation is not easy and is not for everyone. We know that skill is the primary difference between weekend gamblers in Vegas as opposed to the advantage gambling of professional poker players. Professional traders quantify their results and spend plenty of time examining their losses to learn from them, rather than burying their heads in the sand.

We found out why technical analysis works, based on the human desire to create order out of chaos. We found out that technical analysis works best in the absence of fundamental shocks to the market. In other words, all things being equal, technical analysis methods generally give better clues as to market behavior in the future than fundamental analysis; at the same time, fundamentals drive the markets, not technicals. We learned about how we need to use the white space on our charts, the canvas of the technician, to paint a picture of the future with leading indicators. We went through a very brief review of Elliott Wave theory and how it helps us to find trends and counter trends. Despite the claims of some Elliott Wave cult members, we must remember that it is called Elliott Wave *theory*; it is not a fact, as some claim.

No technical method, including Elliott Wave theory, the Gartley trading method, or any other discipline, is perfect 100 percent of the time. The markets are made up of individuals who have free will to do anything they want, including manipulating the markets and breaking "nature's law" if necessary to gain a profit. However, there is definitely a tendency for the market to behave in a certain fashion. These tendencies conform to Elliott Wave theory, Fibonacci ratios, and other technical methods. It is important for us understand the psychology behind the core tools that we will be using to find Gartley Patterns—namely the retracement and extension routines. Together, the retracement tool and the price extension or quadrilateral tool will be the primary tools we will be using as we move forward in this book to help us identify valid Gartley Patterns. However, before we go any further, let's find out more about the man who started it all.

PART II

The Gartley Pattern

T he Gartley Pattern is the most powerful pattern used in the financial markets, and Part Two will convince you of this fact. But before we define the pattern itself, we must give credit where credit is due and discuss the man himself, H.M. Gartley, and the original pattern set forth in his book *Profits in the Stock Market*. We then look at the evolution of the pattern over the past 70 or more years and compare the Gartley Pattern with other classical technical patterns. After reading this section, you might find that you've been trading Gartley Patterns, but you haven't even been aware of it. The chapter concludes with fresh labels for the Gartley Pattern as it relates to the original Gartley material. In Part Three, entitled "Application," we apply the knowledge that we have acquired in Part Two to real-world trading situations.

CHAPTER 4

The Gartley
Pattern Revealed

Harold Gartley was born in Newark, New Jersey in 1899. He received his Bachelor's Degree in commercial science and a Master's Degree in business administration from New York University. Over the years, he worked on Wall Street as a board boy, runner, broker, analyst, financial advisor, and educator. Gartley provided a stock market data newsletter entitled *Gartley's Stock Market Data—A Comprehensive Tabulation of Stock Market Data Digested for the Use of Stock Market Students*. He traveled to give lectures on the subject of technical analysis and privately taught many prominent Wall Street traders.

Gartley's teachings on technical analysis eventually evolved into a course that was published as a 3-ring binder in 1935 and was entitled *Profits in the Stock Market*. Gartley wrote many articles about the stock market, but *Profits in the Stock Market* is considered to be his best work. Fewer than 1,000 copies were originally sold at $1,500 per copy. The selling price of the book was high at the time, given that it cost $500 to buy a new Ford car back then. It's amazing to think that he could sell *any* of these courses at such a steep price in the middle of the Great Depression.

The original Gartley book has become a technical analysis classic and a collector's item. *Profits in the Stock Market* covers a wide array of subjects including trends, Dow theory, triangles, moving averages, and gaps. It is said that Gartley has done more work on the subject of volume analysis in the stock market than anyone else.

Gartley was one of the founders of the New York Society of Security Analysts, and from 1947 until his retirement in 1969, he worked in the field of financial public relations. Harold M. Gartley passed away in 1972 at the age of 73. In 1979, Billy Jones from the Lambert-Gann Publishing Company purchased the copyright from Mrs. Gartley and started publishing *Profits in the Stock Market* as a hardbound, 446-page book. In 1981, the Market Technicians Association gave its annual award posthumously to H.M. Gartley for his contribution to technical analysis.

"ONE OF THE BEST TRADING OPPORTUNITIES"

The pattern that traders refer to today as the Gartley Pattern is discussed in detail in *Profits in the Stock Market* under the heading "One of the Best Trading Opportunities." It is quoted here.

In the life of those who dabble in Wall Street, at some time or other there comes a yearning—"just to buy them right, once, if never again." For those who have patience, the study of top and bottom patterns will provide such an opportunity every now and then—the chance does not arise every day, but when it does, a worthwhile opportunity, with small risk, becomes available. Let us look at Figure 27 (A). When, after an intermediate decline in either a bull or a bear market, such as A-B in the diagram, has proceeded for some time, and activity has shown a definite tendency to dry up, indication that liquidation is terminating, a minor rally like B–C sets in, with volume expanding on the upside. And when a minor decline, after cancelling a third to a half of the preceding minor advance (B–C) comes to a halt, with volume drying up again, a real opportunity is presented to buy stocks, with a stop under the previous low.

In eight out of ten cases wherein each of these specific conditions occurs, a rally, which will provide a worthwhile profit, ensues. In the other two cases, only small losses have to be taken. In trading this formation, the observer is depending upon the probability that either a head-and-shoulders, or double bottom, which are the two reversal patterns which occur most frequently, is developing.

The art in conducting an operation of this kind lies in:

A: Having the patience to wait until a decline of substantial proportions has developed;

B: Observing that all conditions laid down are present;

C: Having the courage to buy just as soon as the minor reaction, which tests the bottom, shows signs of terminating; and

D: Having the courage to get out with a fair profit (10–20 per cent), or at least protect it with stops.

Hourly charts of the averages, available for guiding the operation, repay the market student for all the efforts he puts into keeping them day after day, when they are of less practical use.

Similar opportunities occasionally develop for that small part of the trading fraternity which has the intestinal fortitude and temperament to sell stocks short. The case in reverse is laid out in Section B, of Figure 27."

—Gartley, H.M., *Profits in the Stock Market*, Lambert Gann Publishing, 1935, pp. 221, 222. Reprinted with the permission of the Lambert Gann Publishing Company.

The foregoing text and Figure 4.1 (Figure 27 in Gartley's text), which appear on pages 221 and 222 of *Profits in the Stock Market*, form the basis for anything that is referred to today as a Gartley Pattern.

Understanding why a trading method works is important, because most traders who trade a system they don't understand (such as black boxes) are almost guaranteed to quit using it when they go into a drawdown. Then, they buy another black box, go into a drawdown, quit, then buy another black box, and so on. This insanity will continue until they understand *why* the system works or fails. With this in mind, let's carefully consider each of the individual legs that constitute the Gartley Pattern to understand the psychology behind it.

In Figure 4.1, Gartley first identifies a bearish A–B leg in the first example on the left (A). This leg appears to be a significant trend move or impulsive phase, with minor rallies punctuating the down trend. At the completion of this A–B leg, we notice a significant rally that is labeled as the B–C leg. This B–C rally exceeds the previous rallies in the A–B downtrend in both price and time. This B–C price action indicates that the previous downward trend might be complete and that the B–C leg might be indicating the beginning of a new impulsive trend move in the opposite direction. This B–C leg is typical of what happens when traders all begin to cover their short positions after a sustained bearish trend. The B–C leg terminates when the short covering is complete. With this in mind, the assumption is that the market will not take out the low at point B as a new

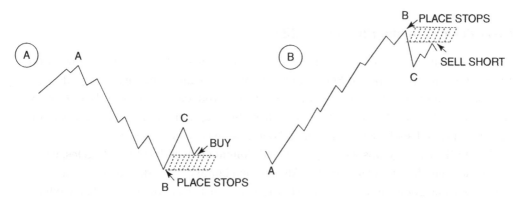

FIGURE 4.1 Diagram from *Profits in the Stock Market*
Source: Gartley, H.M. *Profits in the Stock Market*, Lambert Gann Publishing Company, 1935, p. 222.

trend up will probably continue higher and never look back. Based on this information, Gartley puts his protective sell stop just below point B.

Though Gartley mentions the A–B leg in his book, most teachers of the Gartley Pattern omit this important aspect of the pattern. This additional part of the pattern is discussed further along in this text as the W–X leg. At the completion of the B–C move, Gartley mentions that there will be a minor decline that cancels one-third to one-half of the preceding minor advance (B–C). In other words, Gartley is looking for a 33 to 50 percent retracement of the B–C move up. Why does this minor decline take place? It could be caused by traders who were anxious to go short during the previous A–B decline. These bears were waiting for a significant pullback during the trend down; however, the market kept missing their sell limit orders on the rallies. Now that the market has had a significant rally against the downtrend, they start selling at point C and push the market down. Depending on where they get filled, they will put their stops just above point C. This selling from the "late bears" pushes the market down into what Gartley describes as a minor decline. As we will see, the original Gartley Pattern as described previously ends up having a very different look and feel from the way it is being taught today.

MODERN VERSIONS OF THE PATTERN

My personal experience with the Gartley Pattern started back in the 1990s. An Internet contact referred me to Robert Miner, who was considered to be the authority on all things related to the works of the legendary trader W.D. Gann. I purchased Robert's software Dynamic Trader and found a function that allowed one to quickly determine whether the swings on a chart conformed to a typical Elliott Wave structure or to a G222. I thought to myself, "What in the world is a G222?" After a bit of research, I was led to Larry Pesavento.

Larry Pesavento and the Gartley 222

Larry Pesavento is a veteran trader and an author of over 10 books on trading. In the 1980s, as many *Profits in the Stock Market* books were gathering dust, Larry blew the dust off of his copy and decided it was time to reintroduce the world to H.M. Gartley. Larry coined the term "Gartley 222" in 1984 from the page number in the book where the pattern appears. I spoke with Larry to find out how he came across Gartley's book.

In the 1970s, Larry was working for Conti Commodities in West Los Angeles, which was located just four blocks from the "Alexandrian Library" of trading books at the time, the Investment Center Bookstore. The bookstore owner, Don Mack, gave Larry full access to the store's library. Overwhelmed with the selection of books, Larry asked Don which book he should read first. Don didn't hesitate and told Larry to read *Profits in the Stock Market* by H.M. Gartley.

Gann expert Ernie Quigley of HarmonicTiming.com describes his first meeting with Larry Pesavento as follows:

It seems like it was a lifetime ago, but back in 1992 I visited Larry Pesavento and Jim Twentyman at their trading room in Pismo Beach, California. I had hand charted May soybean prices from the first day of trading on October 5, 1936 to the time I visited them and was sharing with them some of my findings. At that meeting Larry introduced me to the practical use of geometry in trading. One of the patterns Larry shared with me was what he called a "Gartley 222" pattern. He called the pattern this because it was described on page 222 of the book *Profits in the Stock Market* written by H.M. Gartley back in 1935.

Larry first mentioned the Gartley 222 in his book *Astro Cycles: A Traders Perspective*. Larry describes Gartley's book in the following words:

This is the best book on the technical aspects of the stock market that I have ever found. It is interesting that it was written before R.N. Elliott was popularized by Charles Collins. On page "222" of this book is a time and price pattern that is THE best technical trade I have ever found. It has everything that the speculator could ask for in a trade:

1. Control of risk—you place your stop above (below) the old high (low).
2. Trading in the direction of the short term trend—you are not picking a top.
3. The Profit to Loss ratio is better than 4 to 1.
4. Three out of four (75 percent) of the trades will be profitable.

Later in the same book, Larry includes four rules for the Gartley 222.

1. A-B-C Correction.
2. Price at Fibonacci level at point C (.618 retrace).
3. Risk-Reward Level Excellent.
4. Stop Protection quantified at pt. A.

Figure 4.2 shows Larry's initial labeling of the Gartley 222.

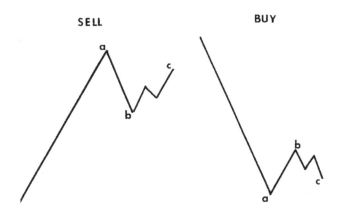

FIGURE 4.2 Labeling the Gartley 222
Source: L. Pesavento, *Astro Cycles: A Trader's Perspective*, Traders Press, 1996, p. 143.

As you can see, Larry's labeling was a departure from Gartley's original labels. Figure 4.3 shows the labeling to display an X before the ABC.

Larry's definition and labeling of the Gartley 222 became more refined when he released his next book, *Planetary Harmonics of Speculative Markets*. In it, he revised his labeling of the Gartley 222 as shown in Figure 4.4.

At this point Larry was looking only for Gartley Patterns to terminate at a .618 Fibonacci retracement of the XA leg. In addition, Larry acknowledges that the formula he was using to calculate the D point (D = B + C − A), comes from Charles L. Lindsay's book *Trident: A Trading Strategy.*

In 1997, Larry Pesavento released another popular book entitled *Fibonacci Ratios with Pattern Recognition*. It was at this point Larry started to include patterns that terminate at both the 61.8 *and* 78.6 percent retracement levels. In addition, Larry changed the formula of the corrective part of the Gartley 222 from Lindsay's D = B + C − A to AB = CD. Larry based his new calculation on a picture from

FIGURE 4.3 XABC Labeling for the Gartley 222
Source: L. Pesavento, *Astro Cycles: A Trader's Perspective*, Traders Press, 1996, p. 144.

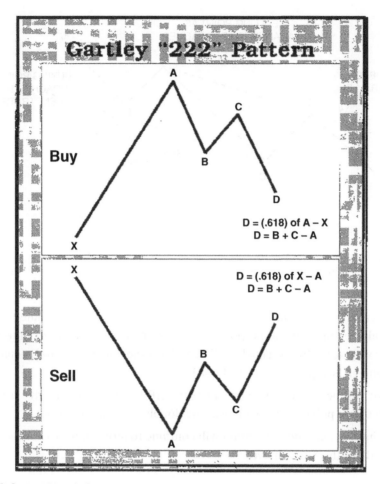

FIGURE 4.4 XABCD Labeling
Source: L. Pesavento, *Planetary Harmonics of Speculative Markets*, Traders Press,1996, p. 38.

Chapter 10 of Gartley's book captioned "Trend Lines." That figure is reprinted here as Figure 4.5.

Larry included more stringent rules for the Gartley 222 in *Fibonacci Ratios with Pattern Recognition*. His six rules for a bullish Gartley 222 are as follows:

1. The swing down from point A will terminate at point D. This will be at the .618 or .786 retracements 75% of the time. The other 25% of the time, the retracements will be .382, .500, or .707.

2. There must be an AB = CD pattern observed in the move from A to D.

3. The BC move will be .618 or .786 of AB. In strongly trending markets expect a .382 or .500 retracement.

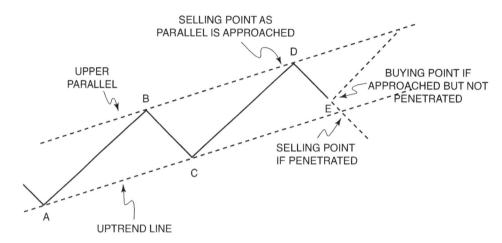

FIGURE 4.5 The Origin of AB = CD
Source: Gartley, H.M. *Profits in the Stock Market*, Lambert-Gann Publishing Company, 1935, p. 249.

4. Analyze the time frames from point X to A and A to D. These time frames will also be in ratio and proportion. For example, the number of time bars up from point X to A is equal to 17 bars. The time bars from A to D equal 11. Seventeen is approximately 1.618 of 11.

5. There will be a few instances where the AB = CD move will give a price objective at point X. This will be a true double bottom formation.

6. If point X is exceeded, the trend will continue to move down to at least 1.27 or 1.618 of the X to A move.

—Pesavento, Larry, *Fibonacci Ratios with Pattern Recognition,*
Traders Press, 1997, p. 56

In *Fibonacci Ratios with Pattern Recognition,* Larry adds some additional criteria to the Gartley 222. According to rule 1, Gartley 222 patterns can complete at any of the internal retracement ratios starting with .382, not just at the .618 ratio as mentioned in *Planetary Harmonics.* However, the distinction is made that the .618 and .786 will appear more frequently. Also, in rule 3 Larry starts to focus on the Fibonacci ratio relationships between the B–C leg and the A–B leg. In addition, time analysis is now mentioned in rule 5. The example used describes a Fibonacci relationship in time between the X–A leg and the A–D leg.

The .786 ratio is mentioned for the first time in Larry's books in *Fibonacci Ratios with Pattern Recognition.* Where did Larry learn about .786?

Bryce Gilmore and Geometry of the Markets

Bryce Gilmore wrote *Geometry of the Markets* in 1989. It was a ground-breaking work in regard to the use of geometry in the financial markets. In it, Bryce introduces the trading world to 1.272, or the square root of 1.618. In his next book, *Geometry of the Markets II*, published in 1993, Gilmore includes the square root of .618 as an important ratio: .786.

Larry Pesavento recalls his first meeting with Bryce Gilmore in 1988:

> Ross, this takes me down memory lane. I was in Chicago with Mark and Markus and they come running up to me to tell me of Bryce Gilmore's lecture—I went to the room and discovered that I was seeing a genius at work in watching and listening to Bryce. We became good friends, and he is responsible for my success like no other person. I miss seeing him as often as we did in the early 1990s in Pismo beach. There is a lot more to this story, but Bryce is the man who brought sacred geometry to the markets. I used the Gartley pattern and called it the Gartley 222 back in 1984, but I did not know the importance of .786 until I met Bryce.

For those of you who are interested, the number 786 is popular for reasons other than trading, especially in the Middle East. The first verse of the Quran states, "In the name of Allah, the Beneficent, the Merciful." When we assign numerical values to the Arabic letters of this verse, guess what number we get? 786.

Scott Carney and Harmonic Trading

One of Larry Pesavento's students, Scott Carney of harmonictrading.com, decided to do some further work on the Gartley Pattern to try to improve its reliability. Carney felt that each leg in a Gartley Pattern should have a specific Fibonacci relationship to the other legs in the pattern. The caveat to this criterion is that these relationships cannot be exact. If we were to wait for a Gartley Pattern with these exact parameters, we would be waiting a long time. Therefore, Scott Carney assigned a certain percent tolerance to each of the legs in his version of the Gartley Pattern.

Scott's rules for the Gartley Pattern were published in his book *Harmonic Trading* in 1999. Scott lays down four rules that he looks for:

1. Precise 61.8 percent B point retracement of the X–A leg.
2. BC projection must not exceed 1.618.
3. Equivalent AB = CD pattern is most common.
4. 0.786 XA retracement.

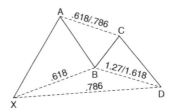

FIGURE 4.6 Scott Carney's Gartley Pattern
Source: Carney, Scott. *Harmonic Trading, Volume One: Profiting from the Natural Order of the Financial Markets*, FT Press, 2010, p. 103. Reprinted with permission.

Figure 4.6 is an illustration of Scott's Gartley Pattern.

As you can see, the pattern is a complex one that conforms to additional rules not described by Larry Pesavento. The main differences between Scott Carney's and Larry Pesavento's Gartley Patterns is that Scott will call it a Gartley only if the D point is at the .786 percent retracement of the X–A leg. In addition Scott wants the B point to complete at the .618 retracement of the X–A leg.

HISTORICAL SUMMARY

As noted at the beginning of this part, the original Gartley Pattern was quite simple. Gartley did not discuss any Fibonacci ratios or Elliott Waves. According to Gartley's original material, all he was looking for was a significant rally off a top or bottom, followed by a retracement of 33 to 50 percent. Based on Gartley's original example, the pattern included only four data points or three legs. It is of interest that the modern version of the Gartley Pattern does not include Gartley's A–B leg.

In Elliott Wave terms, the original pattern would appear to be the completion of a Wave Two. That means we would be trading a Wave Three, a trade that most Elliotticians would consider very difficult to identify. The Gartley Pattern, in the context of the original and modern versions, is simply a trend move followed by a counter-trend move. According to the basics of Elliott Wave theory, we learned that the counter-trend move is made up of overlapping waves, unlike the initial impulse phase that precedes it.

In the original Gartley material, there is no discussion of an ABC zigzag correction. This is all that Gartley said, "And when a minor decline, after cancelling a third to a half of the preceding minor advance (B–C) comes to a halt, with volume drying up again, a real opportunity is presented to buy stocks, with a stop under the previous low." However, the reason that Larry Pesavento included the Elliott A = C or the AB = CD criteria as part of his version of the pattern is the printed example that Gartley displays in Figure 4.1. If we look at this picture again, the B–C move in the bullish example on the left is a straight line, whereas the bearish example on the right includes the AB = CD symmetry. It was based on this bearish example in Gartley's illustration that the AB = CD was added to the pattern by Pesavento.

OBJECTIVE PATTERN CRITERIA

Does the end of the A–B leg have to terminate at the 61.8 percent Fibonacci retracement? Does the end of the B–C leg have to complete on a Fibonacci retracement? In my opinion the answer to both of these questions is No. It's nice to see this, but it's not mandatory. This added criterion filters a significant number of exceptional setups that would still qualify under Pesavento's and Gartley's rules.

One of the aspects of identifying the AB = CD portion of the Gartley Pattern is the B–C leg. How long should the B–C leg be? As with other technical methods, it is subjective. However, there are certain "guidelines" that we should follow. There should be a minimum amount of time for the B–C leg. For example, what if the A–B leg is 50 bars in length and the B–C leg is 2 bars in length? Would the B–C leg qualify as a BC of an AB = CD? The short answer is No, as there should be a minimum amount of time for the B–C leg. There should also be a minimum price. For example, what if AB had a price range of 100 points and BC had a price range of 10 points? Would BC qualify as part of an AB = CD? No. There should be a minimum price retracement of the BC swing. So what minimums do we expect to see for price and time retracements of the A–B leg? Some technicians will be adamant about using a minimum of a 38.2 percent price retracement or a 38.2 percent time retracement of the A–B leg. These minimum thresholds *could be* important minimum numbers that work. However, we must be aware of "analysis paralysis."

Sometimes opportunities are presented, yet they don't conform "perfectly" to our minimum levels. They may be off by a point or a minute. Should we throw the baby out with the bathwater? By no means! Use your brain, train your eye, and visually find an AB = CD that has a certain "look and feel." Sorry, this might not be what you want to hear, but we need to start using the right side of the brain for trading.

One of the most important modern improvements of the Gartley Pattern occurs when the corrective section of the pattern exhibits the AB = CD symmetry. This symmetry of the two waves can be seen in many other classical technical patterns, such as flags, pennants, and triangles. After a breakout from these patterns, the market will often run about the same length as the wave that precedes the consolidation part of the pattern.

In regard to the retracement of the X–A leg, I discovered that the 78.6 percent retracement works very well, especially in a trend-reversal situation. Larry Pesavento observed that the Gartley Pattern appeared to be a more reliable pattern if it completed at a 61.8 percent retracement or a 78.6 percent retracement of the X–A leg of the pattern. Based on my experience with the Gartley Pattern, it appears that if you had to choose between these two ratios, 78.6 percent seems to work the best. Scott Carney narrowed it down even further by saying that it isn't a Gartley *unless* it completes at 78.6.

I would not go as far to say that a 61.8 percent Gartley is not a Gartley, but my preference is to trade only the 78.6 percent Gartley patterns. Why? I would rather trade less often and increase the chances of my wins on the few trades that I make. If you feel a need to trade more often, it may be time for you to take a personal inventory. You might be a "trading junkie," as my friend Robert Miner puts it. Regardless of your style of trading, we need to develop the virtue of patience, to wait for good Gartley Patterns. Remember, Gartley himself said, "The art in conducting an operation of this kind lies in . . . having the patience to wait."

Another benefit of using the 78.6 percent retracement is its proximity to where our protective stop is located. Remember Gartley said, "In the other two cases, only small losses have to be taken." So if we choose the 78.6 percent rather than the 61.8 percent Fibonacci level to enter, our risk will be reduced. How? Remember where we have to put our stop? If we use the location Gartley suggested for our stop, our risk would be less with a 78.6 percent entry than with a 61.8 percent entry. If we are wrong, we risk less money with an entry at 78.6 versus 61.8 percent.

Another reason that I prefer the 78.6 percent level is that the trading public is typically unaware of this level, as it does not appear in the defaults of most Fibonacci retracement drawing tools. Therefore, there is contrarian value in using this level. In addition, by the time a market arrives at 78.6 percent, most of the typical 61.8 percent Fib traders have been stopped out. At this point in time, there is a lot of uncertainty, as traders watch for a bounce or a break based on their focus on the previous high or low.

Also, typically there is an increase in the volatility in the 78.6 percent retracement area as the market begins to reflect the uncertainty of its participants when the market approaches a significant high or low. The volatility in this zone will help us if we enter with a single-in/scale-out strategy; this is discussed in more detail in Part Three, "Application."

RETRACEMENT AND EXTENSION CLUSTERS

Utilizing both the price-retracement and price-extension tools that we learned about in Part One, we now need to look for a "cluster" of these projections. What do we mean by a cluster? When we draw our price retracements and extensions, ideally we would like to see the lines of these tools land very close to each other, if not right on top of each other.

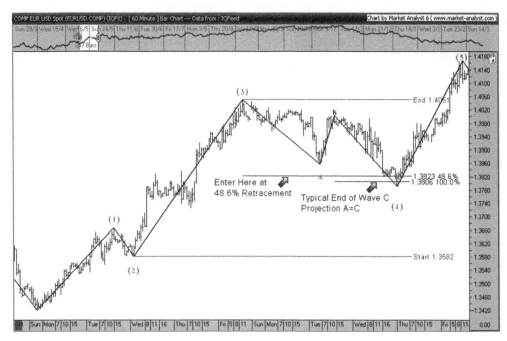

FIGURE 4.7 End of Wave 4 Gartley

However, if the lines are a substantial distance from each other, then the projections create a signal that is unclear. Only when the lines cluster close together do we have a valid signal to buy or sell. An example of a Gartley Pattern completing at the end of Wave 4 can be seen in Figure 4.7. The price retracement and extension lines are landing in a tight cluster where the market finds support.

The clustering concept at first may appear to be very subjective. It is, yet it isn't. The AB = CD projection made with the price-extension tool will give us a clue as to which one of the various Fibonacci levels the market will reverse at. If the AB = CD projection is closer to the 48.6 percent retracement than the other Fibonacci retracement levels, then the bias is toward a Gartley Pattern completing at the 48.6 percent retracement, as seen in Figure 4.7.

In Figure 4.8 we have drawn a 78.6 percent retracement line based on what looks to be an impulsive phase or an XA move down. In the following two Figures we are using the Elliott Wave labels instead of Pesavento's XABCD. Armed with our Fibonacci price-retracement tool, we would first click the high, then the low to display the retracement level as shown in the Figure.

Next we need to confirm that the price-extension tool displays a line that is closer to the 78.6 percent retracement than the other Fibonacci retracement lines. To plot this line we measure Wave A and project it from the end of Wave B; this gives us the end of Wave C price projection. The result can be seen in Figure 4.9.

FIGURE 4.8 78.6 Percent Retracement

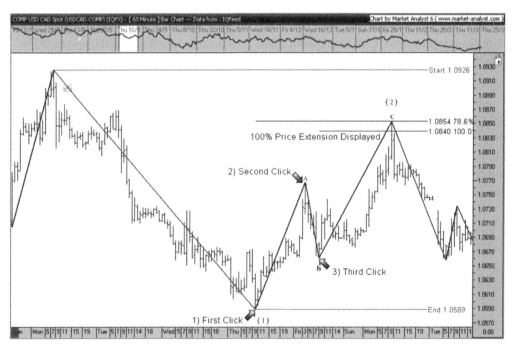

FIGURE 4.9 Cluster of 78.6 Percent Retracement and 100 Percent Extension

FIGURE 4.10 61.8 Percent Gartley Pattern

Based on an entry at the 78.6 percent Fibonacci retracement at 1.0854, we would place our stop just above the beginning of Wave 1. This is a good place to put our stop from an Elliott point of view, because if we were looking to trade a Wave 3, we wouldn't expect the USD/CAD to go beyond the beginning of Wave 1. Does it look as though the USD/CAD turned into a Wave 3? If you are making money on the trade, does the wave count really matter?

An example of a 61.8 percent Gartley Pattern can be seen in Figure 4.10. Notice how the AB = CD price projection line lands just above the 61.8 percent Fibonacci retracement line.

If the AB = CD projection is closer to the 78.6 percent retracement than the other Fibonacci retracement levels, then the bias is toward a Gartley Pattern completing at the 78.6 percent retracement. If the AB = CD price projection lands between the Fibonacci ratios, then the signal is unclear. For example if the AB = CD projection lands right between the 61.8 percent and the 78.6 percent retracements, then there is no bias as to which level the market will reverse at. However, in this case, if the market clearly violates

FIGURE 4.11   100 Percent Gartley Pattern or Double Top

the 61.8 percent level and hits the 78.6 percent level, obviously the 78.6 percent would be the preferred level at which to buy or sell. In the event that the AB = CD price projection lands near the 100 percent retracement level, that indicates that we will have a double top or double bottom. In the past, I referred to this pattern simply as a bullish or bearish retest. The example in Figure 4.11 is a double top or a bearish retest.

In his book, Gartley mentioned that you need courage to trade this pattern. At the retest of a significant high or low, many rookie traders shy away and don't want to trade. If you review Gartley's original bullish example (shown in Figure 4.1) and showed it to an average person on the street and asked them if you should buy or sell, they will almost always tell you to sell. Inherently, this pattern is a contrarian pattern, and it is very difficult to get used to trading it, given that it appears that you are fighting the trend. In addition, volatility typically spikes at the 78.6 percent retracement level when the market approaches a significant high or low. At this point traders get nervous and ask themselves, Will it bounce or break? When you start to trade Gartley Patterns, you will know what Gartley meant when he stated that you need courage; but you will also reap the financial rewards of your newfound bravery!

To recap, in this chapter we considered the history and modern development of the Gartley Pattern. We also studied the most commonly used tools and ratios employed to identify the pattern. In the next chapter we will take a closer look at "Gartley's Gartley" and consider an important aspect of "one of the best trading opportunities" that has been overlooked for over seventy years. . .volume.

CHAPTER 5

Gartley Methods Compared

After reading many books on technical analysis, sometimes we notice that certain methods and tools seem to overlap or complement one another. In this regard, the Gartley Pattern is no exception. You will start to identify Gartley Patterns found in other classical technical patterns such as head and shoulders, flags, pennants, triangles, double tops or bottoms, Elliott Wave, and others. Figure 5.1 shows a typical double bottom on the 60-minute NZD/USD chart.

Now look at this chart one more time and see whether you can find a Gartley Pattern. Can you see it? The pattern is highlighted in Figure 5.2.

Another popular five-point pattern is the head-and-shoulders pattern. The 5-minute chart in Figure 5.3 shows a typical head-and-shoulders pattern in the AUD/USD. In this situation, we would be looking to sell on a break of the neckline that is drawn based on the lows of what Gartley referred to as the APs (armpits). Have a closer look; can you see a bearish Gartley Pattern?

If you can see it, there is a bearish Gartley complete at just above .8700. This level is a much better entry signal for selling than waiting for the break of the neckline down below .8650. The bearish pattern is highlighted in Figure 5.4.

As we will see, Gartley had a very high opinion of the head-and-shoulders and double-bottom or double-top patterns. Those of you who already trade these patterns might want to start looking for Gartley Patterns within these patterns. Adding the Gartley criteria to these classic patterns will definitely improve your trading results.

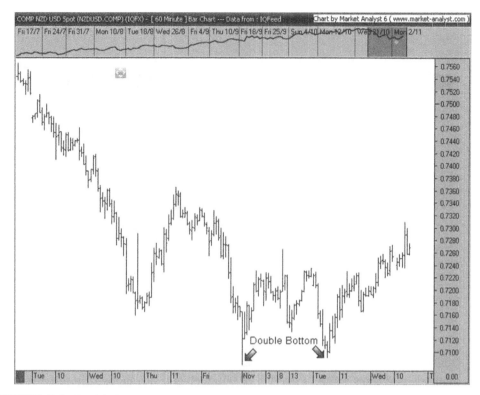

FIGURE 5.1 Double Bottom

FIGURE 5.2 Gartley and the Double Bottom

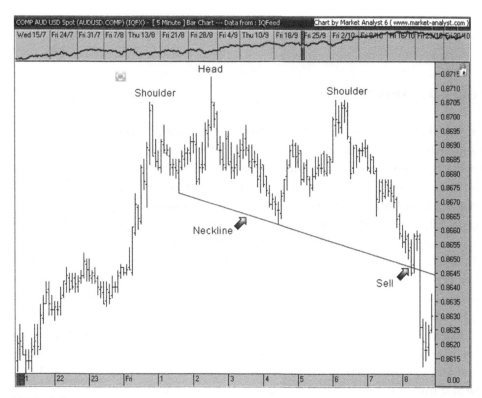

FIGURE 5.3 Head and Shoulders

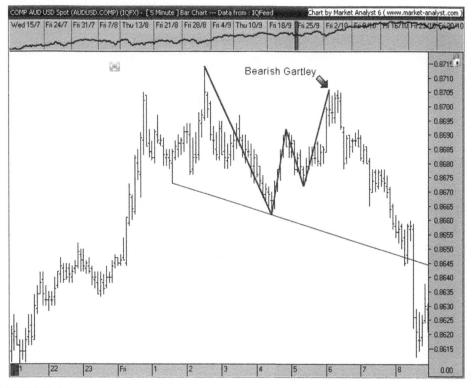

FIGURE 5.4 Gartley and the Head-and-Shoulders Pattern

BACK TO BASICS

Since the reintroduction of the Gartley Pattern to the trading world by Larry Pesavento, many traders have written about it. Apparently, they all have their own unique way of trading it. The situation is not unlike what happened with the popularity of Elliott Wave. Since the trading world has been reintroduced to the "Wave principle," many self-proclaimed Elliott Wave gurus have emerged, each with their own spin on how to trade using the Elliott Wave. Over time, more and more rules were added, and the trade strategy has become much more complicated than what Elliott intended.

In similar fashion, the original Gartley Pattern is very simple compared with its present application. Today, most traders searching for Gartley Patterns ignore some of the original rules that Gartley set forth. In Figure 5.5, we see a pattern that most traders would readily call a "Gartley Pattern." However, Gartley described "an intermediate decline" that must take place before what is labeled as the X point on the chart. The choppiness that precedes the X point of the "Gartley Pattern" is not an intermediate decline. If the chart was shown to H.M. Gartley and he was asked, "Is this what you meant by one of the best trading opportunities?" I'm sure he would say "No."

FIGURE 5.5   Modern Trend-Continuation Gartley Pattern

It's not that the trade shown in Figure 5.5 is a bad trade, but it was not what Gartley was describing in his book. So to review, what are the main differences between the modern Gartley and Gartley's Gartley? The main differences are as follows:

1. The labels in the original pattern are A, B, C. The labels for the modern pattern are X, A, B, C, D.
2. The modern Gartley omits the original A–B leg.
3. The modern Gartley emphasizes the equality AB = CD whereas the original does not.
4. The original Gartley pattern did not include any Fibonacci ratios for retracements, but rather 33 percent and 50 percent.
5. Gartley mentions using volume analysis whereas modern versions do not.
6. The modern Gartley can be a trend-continuation pattern or a trend-reversal pattern. The original was only a trend-reversal pattern (head-and-shoulders or double-top/double-bottom).

On page 223 of his book, Gartley states that of all the patterns he discusses, the four that are "most outstanding and of the greatest value" are the following:

1. The head-and-shoulders reversal.
2. The double reversal.
3. The rounding reversal.
4. The broadening reversal.

In other words, Gartley didn't say that the best pattern in the world was shown in the picture he printed on page 222 of his book; he said that the top two patterns were the head-and-shoulders and the double-top/double-bottom patterns. Gartley's observation is not necessarily a contradiction of his discussion of what he called "One of the Best Trading Opportunities."

The rules he listed for "Gartley's Gartley" are simply rules that improve the results of the head-and-shoulders and the double-top/double-bottom patterns. Remember that he stated on page 221,

> In trading this formation, the observer is depending upon the probability that *either a head-and-shoulders, or double bottom,* which are the two reversal patterns which occur most frequently, is developing.

In view of the foregoing, Gartley's Gartley was either a head-and-shoulders or a double-top or a double-bottom pattern. We have just considered the relationship between the Gartley Pattern and the head-and-shoulders and the double-top/double-bottom in Figures 5.2 and 5.4. In either case, what Gartley was really describing in the picture on page 222 was how to trade the retest of a significant high or low in order to participate in trading a Wave 3.

"ONE OF THE BEST TRADING OPPORTUNITIES" REVISITED

Let's review "One of the Best Trading Opportunities" and look at an example, step by step, including the rules that Gartley included for volume and the intermediate decline he described. First Gartley states,

> When after an intermediate decline, in either a bull or bear market, such as A–B in the diagram, has proceeded for some time, and activity has shown a definite tendency to dry up, indication that liquidation is terminating. . . .

This price behavior can be seen in the chart given in Figure 5.6. We have used the original Gartley labels to avoid confusion. Notice the size of the rallies in the A–B

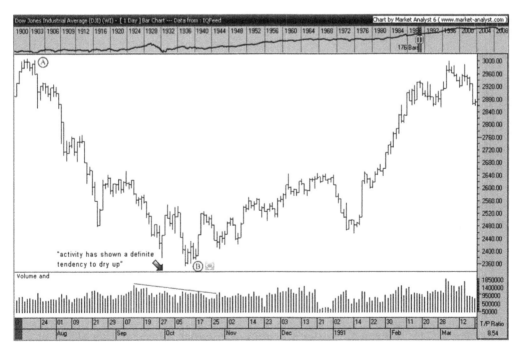

FIGURE 5.6 Intermediate Decline

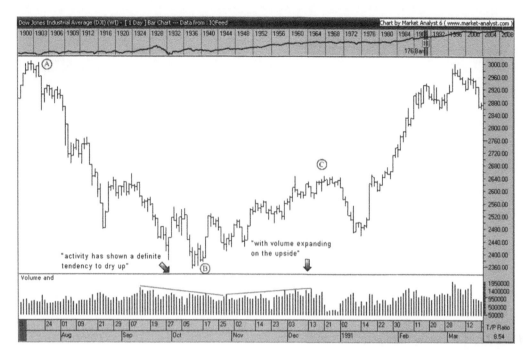

FIGURE 5.7 Minor Rally

decline. It is important to compare these rallies with the coming B–C leg. In addition, we have included volume at the bottom of the chart, just as Gartley included volume analysis in the description of his pattern. Notice the trendline in the volume window. This confirms Gartley's statement that the "activity has shown a definite tendency to dry up."

Next Gartley states that "a minor rally like BC sets in, with volume expanding on the upside." in Figure 5.7, notice the original labeling of the B–C leg along with the increase of volume as indicated by another trendline in the volume window. In addition, what is noticeable here is that the "minor rally" or B–C leg is greater in price and time compared with the previous rallies on the screen. This price-and-time criterion is not mentioned in the text of Gartley's book; however, it is apparent in the diagram on his page 222. An overbalance of price and time of the B–C leg in this situation would indicate that Gartley's B label is a significant low.

Ideally, in Elliott Wave terms, the B–C leg is a Wave 1 of a new impulsive phase. This leg is the most significant part of the pattern when it comes to forecasting future turning points using market geometry. We won't open that can of worms here, but I will discuss this point in detail in my next book.

Gartley then says, "And when a minor decline, after cancelling a third to a half of the preceding minor advance (B–C) comes to a halt, with volume drying up again, a real opportunity is presented to buy stocks, with a stop under the previous low." In Figure 5.8

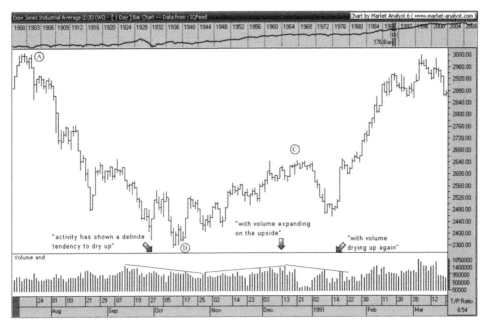

FIGURE 5.8 Minor Decline

notice the decline in volume during the minor decline in price, as indicated by the trend-line on the volume window.

Now let's apply the one-third and one-half retracements that Gartley describes to the example in Figure 5.9.

Gartley mentions placing a stop "under the previous low"; in the preceding case, this would put the stop just below the previous low (highlighted in Figure 5.9 at point B). However, notice that the risk on a trade like this would be significant if we used Gartley's one-third retracement. The suggestion of a one-half retracement as our entry point would reduce the distance and risk between our entry point and our stop. In his book, Gartley makes it clear where his pattern fails, but he is mute when it comes to a definition of a successful trade. In my opinion, if the C point high is taken out with an entry at a 50 percent retracement level, this would signify the completion of a successful Gartley trade setup according to Gartley's setup rules. In the preceding case, you would have a 50/50 chance of the pattern working if it took out the high instead of being stopped out. However, as stated in Part Three, I prefer to use the single-in/scale-out exit strategy. If I had used this strategy in the preceding example, I would have liquidated my second contract by the time the market traded above the C point (more on this later). As you can see in Figure 5.9, the Gartley Pattern would have been successful if you had bought at either a one-third retracement or a one-half retracement.

In view of the preceding discussion, it becomes apparent that the definition of the Gartley Pattern as it is used today is open to interpretation. I believe that the power of

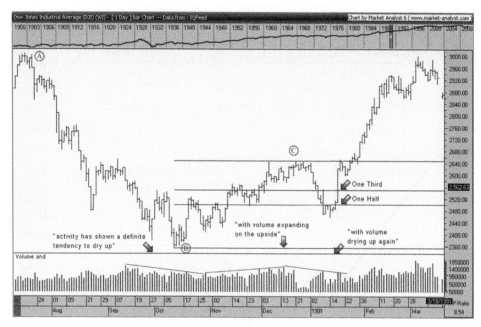

FIGURE 5.9   One-Third and One-Half Retracements

the Gartley Pattern is based on its simplicity. According to Gartley, it was simply a retest of a significant high or low—that's it. Can we refine this general description with some additional tools? Absolutely! If the pattern terminates at a Fibonacci retracement, or if the minor decline subdivides into an AB = CD, or if the pattern conforms to Gartley's rules for volume, even better. The preceding example is the truest example of a Gartley Pattern or what we could call, "Gartley's Gartley." There is no AB = CD, and there are no 61.8 or 78.6 percent retracements.

Before we proceed further, it becomes necessary to separate modern versions of the Gartley Pattern into two groups—trend-continuation Gartleys and trend-reversal Gartleys. In addition, when we consider a trend-reversal Gartley, there currently is no label to identify the "intermediate-decline" phase of the pattern. Therefore we need to modify the current labels of the trend-reversal Gartley to identify this important phase of the original pattern.

NEW LABELING CONVENTIONS

One thing that becomes apparent after looking at Gartley's pattern in *Profits in the Stock Market* is that the labels people use today are different from the labels that Gartley used. Figure 5.10 provides an example of Gartley's labeling.

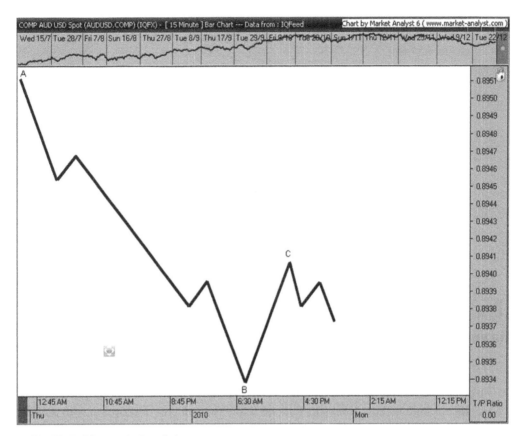

FIGURE 5.10 Gartley's Labels

The Gartley structure presented here is clearly a trend-reversal pattern. As Gartley stated, "in trading this formation, the observer is depending upon the probability that either head-and-shoulders, or a double-bottom, which are the two reversal patterns which occur most frequently, is developing." Therefore, this Gartley Pattern is clearly a trend-reversal pattern, not a trend-continuation pattern. Now compare Gartley's structure and labeling with the structure and labeling of Larry Pesavento. Notice that the Pesavento structure can be either a trend-continuation pattern or a trend-reversal pattern.

Figure 5.11 represents a significant departure from what Gartley was teaching in 1935. The obvious part of the structure that is missing is what Gartley labels as the A–B move. In view of the foregoing, the structure shown here can be either a trend-reversal or trend-continuation pattern.

It is interesting to note that the illustration Gartley uses in his book in both the bullish and bearish pictures appears to be an Elliott Wave five-wave sequence. If you like Elliott Wave, you could re-label Gartley's pattern as it appears in Figure 5.12.

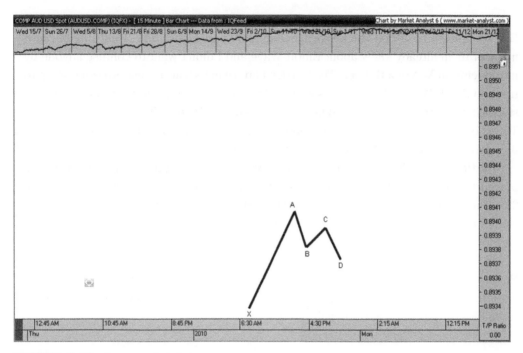

FIGURE 5.11 Pesavento's Labels

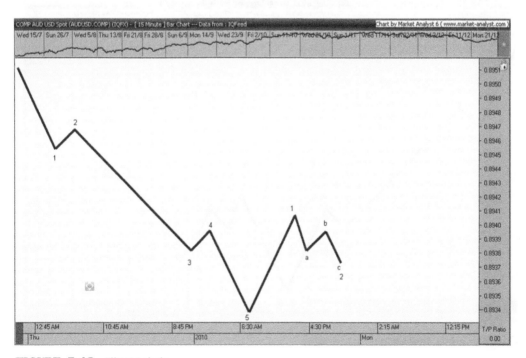

FIGURE 5.12 Elliott Labels

For a number of years I have taught thousands of students around the world the Gartley Pattern based on the above labeling shown in Figure 5.12. I did this because many of them already knew about Elliott Wave and I didn't want to confuse anyone by introducing an X–A or a B–D leg. The Gartley Pattern in its truest sense is a trade setup to trade an Elliott Wave 3. However, as we will discover, at some point most Gartley traders stop using Elliott Wave theory and just trade the Gartley Pattern. To avoid a repeat of the Tower of Babel, it now becomes necessary to introduce labels that are consistent with the current labels (XABCD) for the Gartley Pattern.

Gartley, in his illustration, did not subdivide his A–B leg as we have done in the preceding chart. Therefore, it's an intermediate trend as defined by Gartley on his page 221. If it subdivides into a textbook 5 wave sequence, great; if not, that's okay, too. We are not trading Elliott Wave, we are trading Gartley Patterns. The question is, how should we label this intermediate decline, which Gartley labeled as A–B?

In Figure 5.13, we preserve the current XABCD labeling as presented by Pesavento. However, we have added one additional label, "W," at the beginning of Gartley's original pattern. Overall, the WXABCD pattern is a trend-reversal pattern, one that more closely resembles the pattern that Gartley described.

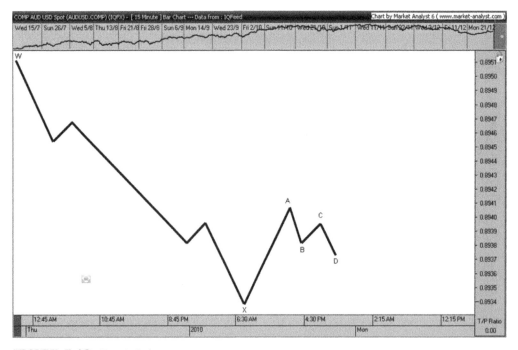

FIGURE 5.13   New Labels

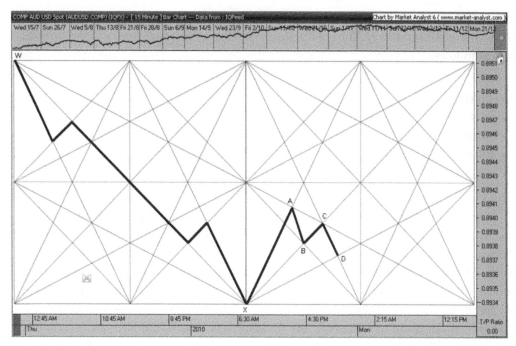

FIGURE 5.14 Gann Boxes

In addition to conforming to Elliott Wave, I noticed that the real key to making this pattern work has to do with angles and the geometry of W.D. Gann. Figure 5.14 provides an example of a Gann Box drawn on the W–X leg and reflected forward. When the Gann Box is adjusted according to the time and price increments of the W–X leg, the market will react more often than not to the angles in the reflected box.

The problem with many technicians is that they want the proverbial silver bullet—a single key that unlocks the mysteries of technical analysis, whether it is the perfect pattern, ratio, oscillator, angle, or planet. The key point to remember is that each market has a different group of traders influencing it. Therefore, you have to use different techniques within different markets. I know this is not what anyone really wants to hear, because it sounds like a lot of work—but who said that being a successful trader would be easy?

WHICH FIBONACCI RATIOS TO USE

The Gartley rules created by Pesavento include the completion of the D point at different Fibonacci ratios. I have found that the best "all-purpose" series of ratios to use for internal retracements on all markets are those mentioned by Bryce Gilmore in his book *Geometry of the Markets II*. The contracting geometric series in *Geometry of the Markets II* is as follows:

- 1.000.
- 0.786.
- 0.618.
- 0.486.
- 0.382.

Any pattern that exhibits an AB = CD where the D point projection lands close to one of the listed Fibonacci ratios can be viewed as a valid Gartley 222, according to Pesavento. I agree, but I always wanted to know whether one of the Fibonacci ratios worked better than the others. I plowed through a number of years of data and had to concur with Scott Carney's opinion that the best Gartleys are the ones that complete at .786. It appears that if one were to trade .618 Gartleys, one could still make money. However, if one were to trade only the .786 Gartleys, one would have an even better success rate. The only problem with waiting for .786 Gartleys is that they don't happen very often in a strongly trending market.

Now that we've clarified the labeling conventions and the proper Fibonacci ratios, let's define the difference between a trend-continuation Gartley (TCG) and a trend-reversal Gartley (TRG).

GARTLEY METHODS COMPARED

As we have seen, there are different types of Gartley Patterns: Gartley's Gartley, Beck's Gartley, Pesavento's Gartley, and Carney's Gartley. Table 5.1 compares the methods.

The first row of Table 5.1 is volume. The rules for volume as described by Gartley are included with Ross Beck's method—not Pesavento's or Carney's.

TABLE 5.1   Comparing the Original Gartley Pattern with Modern Methods

	Gartley	Beck	Pesavento	Carney
Volume	Yes	Yes	No	No
W–X Move	Yes	Yes	No	No
AB = CD	No	Yes	Yes	Yes
Retracement	**33.3, 50**	**38.2,48.6**,61.8,78.6,100	**38.2,50**,61.8,78.6	78.6

The next category is the identification of the intermediate leg described by Gartley (I have labeled this as the W–X leg). The intermediate W–X leg is not identified by Pesavento or Carney.

The next category is the AB = CD. This criterion is included with Beck's, Pesavento's, and Carney's patterns; however, it is not stated specifically by Gartley. In the illustration on page 222 of *Profits in the Stock Market*, Larry Pesavento noticed that the bearish pattern on this page had a clearly defined AB = CD (without the labels); however, the bullish pattern does not include the AB = CD. It appears that the illustration on Gartley's page 222 was not trying to teach us to look for AB = CD, though it does appear with the bearish pattern.

The final category of the table shows which retracements are used. Gartley mentioned only one-third and one-half. Pesavento uses the 50 percent like Gartley but adds 38.2, 61.8, and 78.6 and calls the 100 percent level a true double top or double bottom. I use the same ratios as Pesavento, with the exception that the 50 percent is rather 48.6 percent and the 100 percent level is referred to as a trend-reversal Gartley (TRG) Pattern as explained subsequently. Carney will consider a pattern only if the D point completes at a 78.6 percent retracement of an X–A move.

TREND CONTINUATION

Most traders who refer to Gartley Patterns these days are referring to TCG Patterns. These trade setups are not attempting trend-reversal trades. Notice that volume analysis and the W–X leg are absent.

It's important to consider the pattern rules as they relate to trend continuation. When there appears to be a corrective phase, such as an Elliott Wave 4 taking place during an impulsive phase, then look for the following:

1. AB = CD is apparent in the corrective phase.
2. AB = CD price projection clusters appear with one of the ratios given in the following list.
3. Stop at X.

The price-extension target (AB = CD) must land near one of the following Fibonacci retracements of the XA move:

- .382—**TCG382** (trend-continuation Gartley at 38.2 percent).
- .486—**TCG486** (trend-continuation Gartley at 48.6 percent).

- .618—**TCG618** (trend-continuation Gartley at 61.8 percent).
- .786—**TCG786** (trend-continuation Gartley at 78.6 percent).
- 1.00—**TCG100** (trend-continuation Gartley at 100 percent).

In the next four figures we will consider some examples of trend-continuation Gartley Patterns. For our price-extension tool we will use the quadrilateral as described in Part One. In Figure 5.15, we see the end of the quadrilateral "clustering" with the 38.2 percent Fibonacci retracement. This chart displays a bullish TCG382.

In Figure 5.16, the quadrilateral is very close to the 48.6 percent Fibonacci retracement to let us know that we expect the completion of a bullish TCG486.

In Figure 5.17, the quadrilateral points to just above the 61.8 percent Fibonacci retracement to indicate a bullish TCG618.

Our last example is a bearish TCG786, shown in Figure 5.18.

TREND REVERSALS

A TRG is the pattern that most correctly reflects the rules of H.M. Gartley's "One of the Best Trading Opportunities." It is always a trend reversal trade attempting to trade an

FIGURE 5.15 TCG382

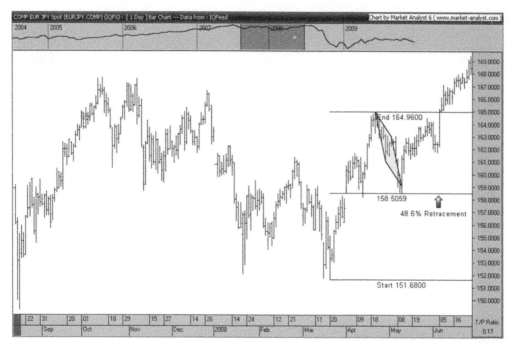

FIGURE 5.16 TCG486

FIGURE 5.17 TCG618

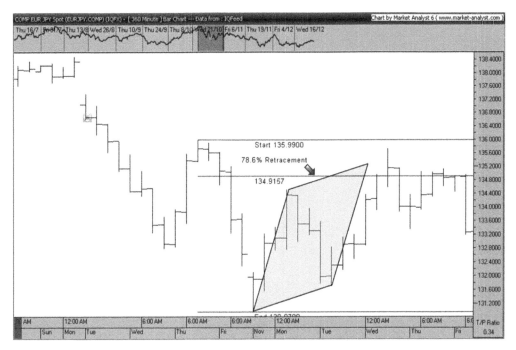

FIGURE 5.18   TCG786

Elliott Wave 3. As instructed by Gartley, we will use volume analysis as part of the TRG trade setup. Though Gartley mentioned the one-third to one-half retracements, we are including the deep retracements of 78.6 and 100 percent. Even though these numbers are a deviation from Gartley's original instructions, the TRG pattern will often occur with a head-and-shoulders pattern or a double-top/double-bottom at these numbers. We are looking for a significant trend (W–X) prior to the completion of the XABCD pattern. The TRG setup is my personal favorite, especially the TRG786.

The pattern rules for trend reversals are as follows:

1. Trend (W–X) appears to have terminated at X. A recent impulsive move (X–A) in the opposite direction of the trend is greater in price and time compared with previous swings in the W–X move.
2. AB = CD is apparent in the corrective phase.
3. AB = CD price projection clusters appear with one of the ratios given in the following list.
4. Stop at X.

The price-extension target (AB = CD) must land near one of the following Fibonacci retracements of the XA move:

- .382—**TRG382** (trend-reversal Gartley at 38.2 percent).
- .486—**TRG486** (trend-reversal Gartley at 48.6 percent).
- .618—**TRG618** (trend-reversal Gartley at 61.8 percent).
- .786—**TRG786** (trend-reversal Gartley at 78.6 percent).
- 1.00—**TRG100** (trend-reversal Gartley at 100 percent).

The volume rules for trend reversals are as follows:

1. Decline in volume as the W–X leg progresses.
2. Spike in volume during the X–A move.
3. Shrinking volume on the A–D move.

We will consider some examples of TRG patterns in the case studies section of Part Three, entitled "Application."

THE BOTTOM LINE

In Part Two we have reviewed the history of the Gartley Pattern. The visibility of the Gartley Pattern was spearheaded by Larry Pesavento with the addition of Fibonacci ratios and the AB = CD. As noted, the pattern as it is described today could be either a trend-continuation pattern or a trend-reversal pattern. As the description of "One of the Best Trading Opportunities" is only of a trend-reversal pattern, it becomes necessary to create two categories of Gartley Patterns—a trend-continuation Gartley (TCG) and a trend-reversal Gartley (TRG). Additional elements mentioned by Gartley have been added by the author to the TRG pattern. These elements include volume analysis and the addition of the W–X leg. The addition of these two original rules makes the TRG more closely resemble the original material printed in 1935 in *Profits in the Stock Market*.

PART III

Application

In Part Three, we first discuss the various ways to initiate positions with the Gartley Pattern. Thereafter, we cover exit strategies along with some basic risk management concepts. Armed with the ability to identify a basic Gartley Pattern with specific entry and exit strategies, we consider a number of real examples of Gartley Pattern trades that were identified during 2009.

CHAPTER 6

Entry and Exit Strategies

Now that we have learned to identify a Gartley Pattern with the clustering of price retracements and extensions, what conclusive evidence do we need to prove that the pattern setup is complete? It is complete when the market touches the Fibonacci retracement level (not the Fibonacci extension level). As we know, there is a difference between a trade setup and a trade entry. Just because a Gartley Pattern setup is complete does not mean that our order has been executed. We will now consider a few methods of entering the market after the completion of a Gartley setup.

ENTRY STRATEGIES

Entry methods really depend on our individual trading style. Some of us like to wait for confirmation; others prefer to be a bit more aggressive. For this reason, we will consider four differing methods to enter a trade once a Gartley Pattern completes: the Fibonacci entry method, the 1-bar reversal entry method, the candlestick entry method, and the technical indicator entry method. We will be looking at the same bearish Gartley Pattern in October 2009 sugar in all four examples to compare the differences.

Fibonacci Entry Method

Our first entry method simply consists of entering the market with limit orders at the exact number of our Fibonacci retracement level. The benefit of this method is that the fill price is typically better than would be with other methods that wait for a move

FIGURE 6.1 Fibonacci Entry Method

in the direction of the trend. The downside to this strategy is that if the market doesn't show any sign of reversing at your Fibonacci retracement level, you will be filled and then quickly stopped out at the point where the Gartley Pattern fails. In the sugar example in Figure 6.1, we would have identified a bearish Gartley prior to its completion and placed limit orders to sell at the 78.6 percent retracement. When the market touched this level, we would have been filled at the 78.6 percent level and would have then placed our initial protective stop just above the high where the Gartley Pattern begins.

1-Bar Reversal Entry Method

Our second entry method is using a 1-bar reversal. The benefit of this entry is that you would get filled only if the market clearly reverses where you expect it to. If the market rips right through your Fibonacci level without stopping and the pattern fails, you will not get filled. However, the downside to this strategy is that when you do get filled on a 1-bar reversal, the fill price is typically not as good as it would be if you simply buy or sell on the Fibonacci retracement number. This is especially true if the range of the bar under consideration was significant. The 1-bar reversal entry method is similar to the 3-bar trailing stop, which we will cover under exit strategies. The obvious difference is that the 1-bar reversal is an entry strategy, whereas the 3-bar trailing stop is an exit strategy.

In the example in Figure 6.2, I've kept the horizontal line visible for the 78.6 percent retracement and put in an arrow pointing to where you would have sold with the Fibonacci limit entry as shown in Figure 6.1. In addition, I have included the 1-bar reversal entry. The rules for the 1-bar reversal entry in Figure 6.2 are as follows:

1. Wait for the market to touch the Fibonacci retracement level.

2. Sell one point below the lowest low of the previous bar.

3. If the previous bar is an "inside bar," ignore it and use the lowest low of the bar before it.

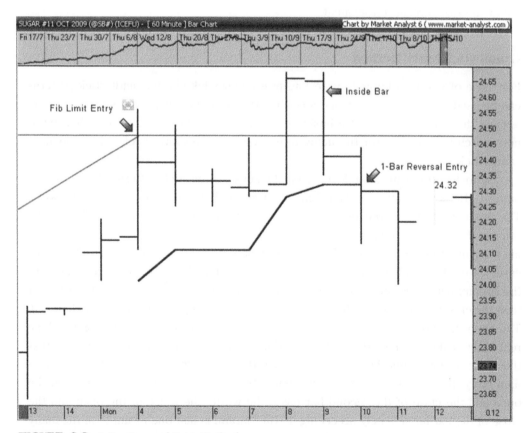

FIGURE 6.2 1-Bar Reversal Entry Method

Of course, remember to reverse these rules for long trades. Also, remember not to consider a bar in the preceding calculation until the bar has finished painting itself on your chart.

What is an inside bar? In Figure 6.2 we have an example of a bar that has been labeled as an inside bar. An inside bar is one where the low of the bar is above or equal to the low of the bar that immediately precedes it and the high of the bar is below or equal to the high that immediately precedes it. Note that we don't compare the highs and lows of the bar under consideration with the highs and lows of any other bar except the bar that is *immediately to the left* of the original bar.

If we were looking to enter the market with a 1-bar reversal entry method at the point indicated on the chart in Figure 6.2, where would we have been filled?

As you can see, we plotted an automatic 1-bar reversal line in Market Analyst to show where the 1-bar reversal entry method would be located. After sugar hit the 78.6 percent retracement, the following two bars were consecutive inside days. Notice how the entry indicator flatlined as it disregarded those two bars. Finally we were filled at 24.32, just below the 78.6 percent retracement.

Candlestick Entry Method

For those of you who know how to interpret candlestick charts, candlestick patterns can be used for entry signals when a Gartley Pattern completes. At this point, we will assume that you have at least a basic knowledge of Japanese candlestick charting. If not, search the Internet for the many free educational resources related to Japanese candlesticks.

Figure 6.3 shows an example of a 2-bar Japanese candlestick pattern called a Harami pattern. "Harami" means "pregnant" in Japanese (and "bastard" in Hindi, by the way). The first candlestick of our bearish Harami pattern is called the mother. The closing price of the mother candlestick is above the opening price. The range between the opening price and the closing price of the candlestick is referred to as the real body; in this case, it would typically be colored white or green on the chart. The next candlestick of the Harami pattern is referred to as the baby. The opening price of the baby is higher than the closing price, and in this case the color of the baby's real body is black or red. The important point of this pattern is that the real body of the baby is "inside" of the real body of the mother—thus the name Harami. The idea behind this pattern is that the range of the second bar is narrower than that of the first, and to follow the pregnant story, the baby bar is causing a "contraction." Therefore, the range between the open and the close of the second bar has to be within the range of the open and the close of the bar immediately preceding it. The Harami is just one example of the many candlestick patterns that one could use to enter the market after the completion of a Gartley Pattern.

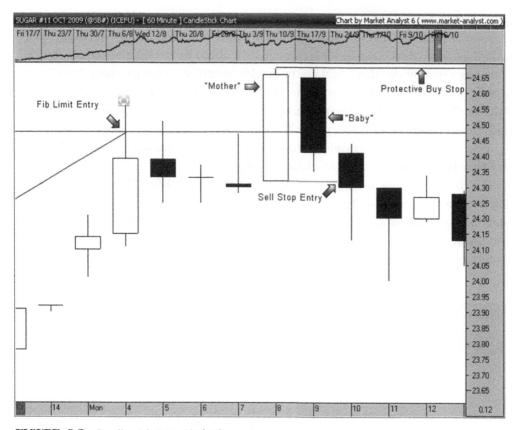

FIGURE 6.3 Candlestick Entry Method

To use a Harami candlestick reversal on a bullish Gartley Pattern, follow these steps:

1. Wait for the market to touch our Fibonacci retracement level.
2. Wait for the completion of a Harami candlestick pattern.
3. Buy one point above the high of the mother. Place your stop one point below the low of the mother.

If you have a preference for certain Japanese candlestick patterns over others, just make sure that the candlestick patterns that you choose to use for entering the market are clearly identified in your trading plan.

Technical Indicator Entry Method

Indicators by their nature are lagging. Often by the time the indicator has generated a buy or sell signal, other trading strategies could have already liquidated positions for a profit. This is a reminder that we need to focus on the optimal settings for an indicator to ensure that the buy and sell signals generated are not too slow. However, despite their limitations, indicators can add value through their ability to identify the current rhythm of the market, a rhythm that might not be quickly identified on a price chart. The choice of indicator or oscillator to use with the Gartley Pattern will be left up to the individual, if this method of entering the market is to be used at all. The important point is that the trader understands the indicator or oscillator well and has absolute confidence in it.

For the purposes of the example shown in Figure 6.4, let's assume that your favorite oscillator is the stochastic. The stochastic oscillator measures where closing prices are relative to the high–low price range over a given number of bars. The oscillator is displayed below the chart as a line with readings ranging from 0 percent to 100 percent. In addition, the oscillator includes horizontal lines that identify the 20 percent and 80 percent levels. One way to use the stochastic is to buy when the stochastic crosses above the 20 percent line and to sell when it crosses below the 80 percent line.

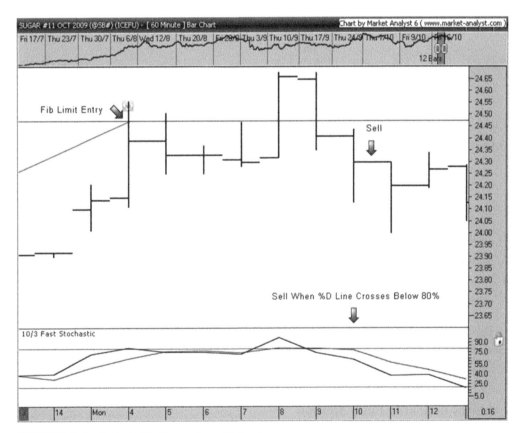

FIGURE 6.4 Technical Indicator Entry Method

In view of the foregoing, we could use the stochastic oscillator to enter the market at the completion of a Gartley Pattern in the following manner:

1. Wait for the market to touch the Fibonacci retracement level.
2. Buy at the market when the stochastic oscillator %D crosses above the 20 percent or sell if it crosses below the 80 percent level.
3. Place your stop just below the previous swing high or low.

The stochastic oscillator is just one example of the many indicators and oscillators that you may choose from to enter the market after the completion of a Gartley Pattern. The example in Figure 6.4 shows where our signal to sell is generated by the %D line.

EXIT STRATEGIES

Where do we make the money—on the entry or on the exit? We know the answer, but then why do we want to spend so much time looking for the ultimate entry signal if it is the exit that makes us money? I believe it is our personal programming from previous trades. Is it not true that every time we put a trade on, we get a very special feeling that maybe this time it's going to be different, maybe this trade is going to be *the one*? We've read about so many successful traders that we rationalize that maybe it just might be our turn this time. There is often a special feeling that traders get when they put a new position on—a high. They are high on "hopium," because they *hope* that they are going to win this time.

Let's compare this new trade high with the programming we have received when exiting those same positions. Looking back, can you think of a single time when you initiated a trade that you felt so sick to the stomach that you wanted to vomit? I didn't think so. But have you ever experienced discomfort, a deer-in-the-headlights feeling, nausea, or even vomiting when you had to take positions off? (I'm sorry; you veterans are probably feeling sick just reading this because I'm feeling sick writing it.) I'm sure that you've had more grief liquidating positions than initiating them. We all have been programmed subconsciously to be more interested in learning about entering a position (euphoria) than exiting a position (nausea). Albert Gray summed it up when he said, "Winners have simply formed the habit of doing things losers don't like to do."

Trading is not easy, otherwise everyone would be doing it. We've established that liquidating a position is not as much fun as initiating it, and when it's a losing position, it's even worse. But how about when you liquidate a trade at breakeven? You might think, that was a waste of time; I could have left my money in T-bills and avoided all the time and stress involved with finding this trade. What about the trades where you make money? Even then we have a tendency to be too hard on ourselves. After liquidating a position for a profit, how often have you ever looked at the chart a week or two later only to see that you could have made a lot more money if you had left the trade on? Then we chastise ourselves and beat ourselves up for not having liquidated the position at the exact high or low on the chart. So even when we make money, our greed might kick in and we will beat ourselves up even when we are profitable.

Win, lose, or draw, trading can be a very painful process for a lot of us and can be a psychological no-win situation. One way I cope with this aspect of trading is not to *expect* a profit on any single trade. The retort is typically, why would you be trading a system where you expect to lose? It's true that Gartley Patterns have a high probability of winning; however, when I put a trade on, I *mentally* expect to lose on that one trade. Therefore, if I do lose, I don't suffer as much mentally, because the trade did what I expected. If it breaks even, I am happy because it did better than "expected," and if I win, I am ecstatic.

Let's compare this attitude with the attitude of those who expect to win on every trade. If they win, they will almost always conclude that they wished they had made more money on the trade, so typically they are disappointed. If they break even, they are disappointed because they expected to make money; if they lose, they feel horrible. Can you see the difference between the two mindsets? The second example, and the one that is most common, is pretty much a no-win situation. In view of the foregoing, by applying the suggestion to "mentally expect to lose" you will be better equipped psychologically the next time you liquidate a position.

3-Bar Trailing Stop

The 3-bar trailing stop is a useful mechanical device to liquidate an open position in an orderly and disciplined manner. There are many mechanical trailing stops available that may work better in a particular market that a student may choose than the 3-bar trailing stop. However, we will cover this method, because it is a good "all-purpose" stop that can be used in any market.

To calculate a 3-bar trailing stop, look at the last three complete bars displayed on the chart. Complete bars are those that are static or are not still in the process of being painted on a chart. If your position is long, you will be looking for the lowest low of the last three complete bars. If you are short, you will be looking for the highest high of the last three complete bars. It is just beyond this high or low that you will place your stop. Typically, we will put a stop one tick beyond this high or low bar. The only caveat to these rules is that you cannot include inside bars in your calculation of the previous three complete bars. An inside bar is a bar where the range from the high to the low is within the range of the bar that immediately precedes it. Remember it can be an inside bar only in relation to the bar immediately to its left, not in relation to the bar two bars ago or three bars ago—only the one to its immediate left.

Here is a reminder for candlestick traders—we do not care about the opening and closing prices with this trailing stop; it considers only the extreme highs and lows, not the opening and closing prices. An example of an inside bar can be seen in Figure 6.5; notice that the range of the bar that is marked as an inside bar is inside of the range of the bar that is labeled as bar 2.

In Figure 6.5 we are going to calculate a 3-bar trailing stop on a short trade. Working from right to left we are going to count back three bars and label them on the chart. The first bar on the right we will label as bar 1 as this is the last complete bar on the chart.

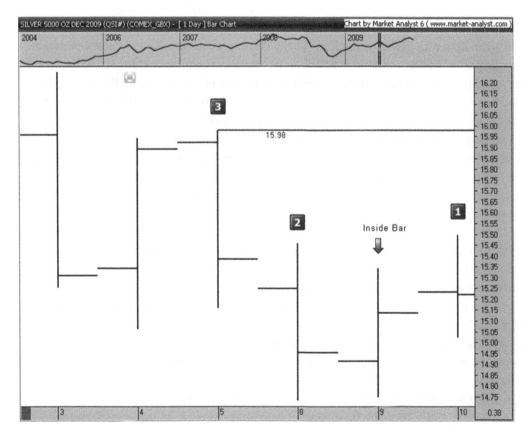

FIGURE 6.5　3-Bar Trailing Stop with Inside Bar

The chart is daily, and regardless of whether a new bar starts to paint on the chart, we will not use any of that new information in the calculation of our stops. Notice that bar number one is not an inside bar, so we will label this bar as the first bar of three. Working from right to left, notice that the bar immediately to the left of bar 1 is an inside bar, so we will not include that bar in the 3-bar count. Working again from right to left, we see that the next bar is not an inside bar, so we will label that one as bar 2. Proceeding to the next bar to the left of bar number 2, we find a bar that is not inside the range of the bar beside it, so we can count that bar as bar 3.

As mentioned, we are short in this silver trade, and we now need to find the highest of the three bars that we have labeled. As you can see, bar 3 is the highest high of the three bars in question, so this will be the place to put a stop. The assumption is that the downtrend would be over if the market takes out the high of bar 3.

One piece of advice: Don't put your stop exactly one tick beyond the range of the bar if the number ends with a 5 or a 0. Put it just beyond the range of the 3-bar high or low and pick unusual numbers that people don't typically use, such as 67 or 74 or 38. This reminds me of bidding on eBay. If you've ever bid on something on eBay, have you ever lost to someone that outbid you by one cent? This happens when we put in a maximum bid on an item with a number such as $20.00. The experienced "eBayer" knows that some inexperienced bidders will bid at $20.00 so he puts in a maximum bid for $20.01 and wins by a penny. This also happens with trading. So in view of the foregoing, if you were long and thinking of putting a sell stop in at $20.00, change it to $19.86 or $19.93 or some other random number to avoid getting stopped out unnecessarily.

Going forward, as new bars continue to be added to the right side of the chart, there will be a need to recalculate our 3-bar trailing stop to determine whether the stop is still on the highest high of the previous three bars. Eventually, the market will exceed the highest high of the previous three bars, and you will be stopped out. The result of the trailing stop that we initiated in the foregoing trade can be seen in Figure 6.6. I left the 1, 2, 3 labels on the screen so that you can see where we put the trade on. The crooked line displayed above the highs is an automatic 3-bar trailing stop available as part of the Beck Tool Group add-on module available through Market Analyst. In this example you would have been stopped out based on the high of June 22, 2009.

Let's look at another example, and this time we will be long. In the example in Figure 6.7, we have a few inside days that have to be ignored with the resulting 3-bar count. The lowest low this time is on bar number two, and the protective sell stopped is placed at 12.48. Remember not to assume that the stop will always be based on the third bar.

Imagine now that we have initiated a long position and that your protective sell stop is in place at 12.48. Now the fresh market data starts to print on the screen, and then it starts to trade lower.

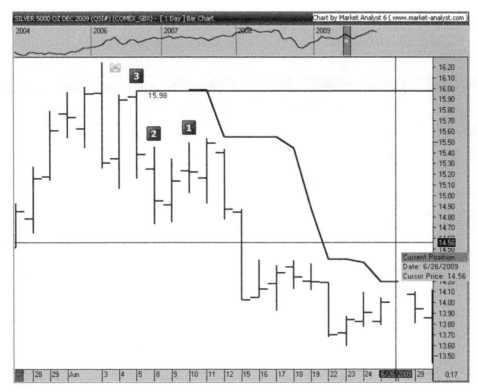

FIGURE 6.6 3-Bar Trailing Stop Indicator

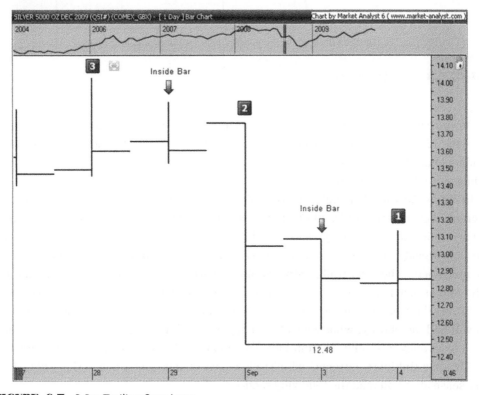

FIGURE 6.7 3-Bar Trailing Stop Long

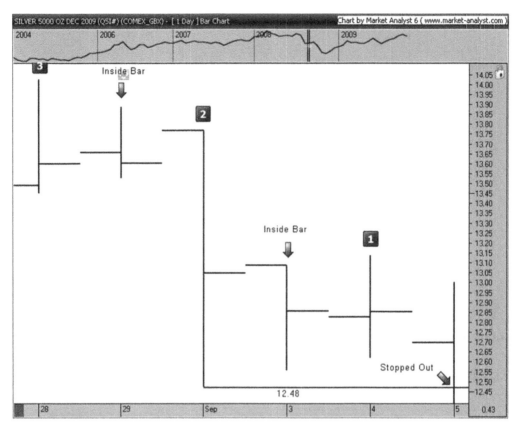

FIGURE 6.8 3-Bar Stopped Out

As you can see in Figure 6.8, we were "long and wrong" and immediately got stopped out at the 12.48 level on the very next bar. As you will see under the next text heading, "Trading Multiple Contracts," we will be using the 3-bar trailing stop in conjunction with trading more than one contract.

In Figure 6.9, the 3-bar trailing stop would have served us well. However, look at the difference between the trades in Figures 6.9 and 6.10. Figure 6.9 is an example of using a 3-bar trailing stop on a daily chart, and Figure 6.10 is an example of a 3-bar trailing stop on a weekly chart. We initiated a TRG786 at the same point on both charts. See how much better the 3-bar trailing stop would have worked on the weekly instead of the daily? Rather than liquidating the position at .7217 on the daily, we would have liquidated at .7675 on the weekly. The two charts are identical except for the time frame, and, as you will find out shortly, what we will be doing is switching gears in the middle of our trades from daily to weekly or from intraday to daily. After we hit our first two targets (see "Trading Multiple Contracts," which follows) we change time frames. This will make more sense after you read the following section.

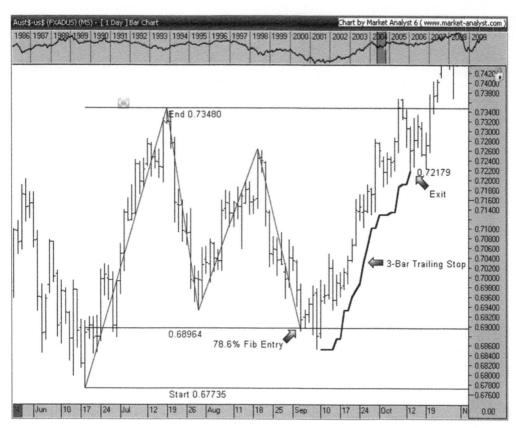

FIGURE 6.9 3-Bar Trailing Stop on a Daily Chart

TRADING MULTIPLE CONTRACTS

There are many different methods of trade management, and it is a personal preference as to which one an individual chooses. In this section we will discuss two methods of trade management. Both methods include trading with multiple contracts.

The first method we call single in/scale out. The single in/scale out strategy dictates that we enter with a minimum of three contracts at a single price; thereafter, we "scale out" or liquidate positions in thirds.

The second method we call scale in/single out. The scale in/single out strategy is a pure martingale and will double the position size at specified intervals if the position moves against us. Once the position moves in our favor by a single interval, we will liquidate all open positions. The scale in/single out strategy is very aggressive, but it has the highest probability of winning.

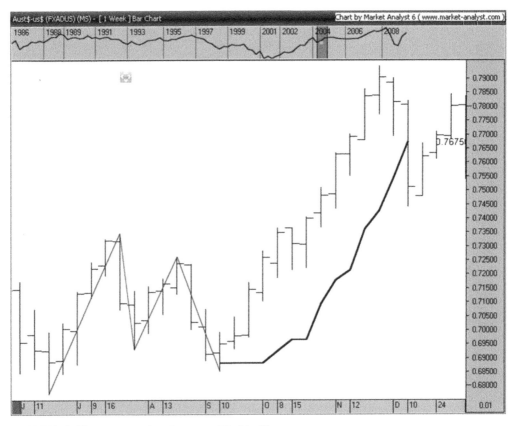

FIGURE 6.10   3-Bar Trailing Stop on a Weekly Chart

Single In/Scale Out

"What type of trader are you? Are you a position trader, a swing trader, or a day trader?" After trying a few different trading styles, we may answer, "I'm a swing trader." Our decision as to what style of trading we choose is often based on our personal preference and our risk tolerance. Each style has its own benefits and drawbacks. For example, the benefit of trading as a day trader is that you are always flat (no positions) at the end of the trading session. In addition, a day trader will get immediate results every day, quick profits earned by scalping the market. The downside to the day traders' style is that they will never enjoy the possibility of a "ten bagger" (to steal Peter Lynch's description of increasing an initial investment tenfold) like a position trader.

On the other end of the trading style spectrum is the position trader. This style of trading involves keeping a trade on for weeks to months with the hope of capturing a major trend move. The benefits to this style of trading are obvious; it is possible as a position trader to have one of those windfall trades where a $1,000 investment yields

$10,000. The downside to being a position trader is that often the risk on the stops is significant compared with the risk taken by a day trader, who may have tight stops. Furthermore, the position trader will often have to lose several times in a row before arriving at the "windfall" trade.

In addition, there are the moderate swing traders who fit neatly between the day traders and the position traders. These traders like to hold on to a trade anywhere from a few days to perhaps a few weeks. They select the "middle way" (are Buddhists swing traders?)—moderate risk, moderate return.

Most traders eventually find that the middle way of the swing trader suits them best. However, because swing traders sometimes hold trades overnight, they may awake to see that the significant profit of the previous session has evaporated; "Oh, if only I were a day trader!" they may lament. Or sometimes a swing trader may liquidate a position after a few days only to notice that if he had left the same position on for six months, he could have retired; his lament is "Oh, if only I were a position trader!" If you have had these feelings, you are not alone. The answer to this dilemma is to trade with the single in/scale out strategy. The single in/scale out strategy allows you to increase return and reduce risk at the same time.

The single in/scale out strategy allows you the flexibility to have different exit rules for each of the contracts that you have bought or sold. The exit rules for one of the contracts will be "day trader" rules. With the day trader contract, you will quickly be in and out of the market, usually intraday, for a quick profit. Another contract will have "swing trader exit rules"; you will hopefully keep this position on for a day or two or longer to secure additional profits not obtained by the day trader contract. You will also have a contract that will have a "position trader" style of exit. Though this contract doesn't pay out often, when it does, it is significant. (I sometimes refer to this contract as the "lottery ticket contract.")

The single in/scale out strategy works best when entering a position where you know what your initial risk is. If you use market orders with your trading strategy, you won't know what your initial risk is until you get filled, even if your stop level is clearly defined. Ideally, we want to use limit orders and clearly defined stops when using the single in/scale out strategy.

Here are the simple rules for the single in/scale out strategy:

1. **Buy or sell three contracts (or more in multiples of three) at your limit price.** Use a single protective stop on all three contracts. The difference between your entry and your stop is your "initial risk."

2. **Calculate your first target.** Your first target is 50 percent of your initial risk. Liquidate one position at this level. If you hit your first target, move your protective stop on the remaining two contracts in the direction of the trade by 50 percent of your initial risk.

3. **Calculate your second target.** Your second target is 100 percent of your initial risk. Liquidate one position at this level. If you hit your second target, move your protective stop on the remaining contract to your entry point.

4. **Manage your last position with a trailing stop.** Use a 3-bar trailing stop or some other volatility-based trailing stop on your last contract as long as the trailing stop is not above (for short trades) or below (for long trades) your entry price. In other words, the worst-case scenario with the last contract is getting stopped out at your entry price without a loss. Once you have one contract left, increase the time frame on the chart for your trailing stop. If you initiated your position on an intraday chart, change the time frame for your trailing stop to a daily chart. If using a daily chart, change to a weekly, and so on.

Let's look at the example in Figure 6.11 of the single in/scale out strategy. In this example we have a bullish TCG786 pattern on a daily chart of the AUD/USD spot Forex.

FIGURE 6.11 Single In/Scale Out Targets

We will be using the Fib entry method at the 78.6 percent retracement at .6910, and the initial protective stop is set to just below the beginning of the Gartley Pattern at .6760. The risk on this trade is theoretically set at 150 points per contract. As discussed, we will be buying three contracts, which means our initial risk for all three contracts is 450 points. Remember to keep within our risk parameters.

Now that we have our risk defined, we need to set our profit targets. To calculate your first profit target, simply subtract your stop price from your entry price. This price differential will define the initial risk per contract. The first target price is 50 percent of your initial risk. In the following example, the initial risk is 150 points per contract. The first target would be 50 percent of 150 or 75 points. If you add 75 to .6910, you get .6985, as seen on the chart. The second target is equivalent to 100 percent of our initial risk. Since our initial risk per contract is 150, we can calculate our second target by adding 150 points to our entry price of .6910 to give us .7060.

Let's assume that we have been filled at .6910 on Figure 6.11. The worst-case scenario after our fill would be that the market drops like a stone and we get stopped out at .6760 and lose 450 points. However, the likelihood of that event is low. Why? Because the most probable event in this situation is that the AUD/USD will hit your profit target first. The reason for that outcome is not due to the magic of the Gartley Pattern but rather to cold hard statistics. Once the position is filled at .6910, there is a higher probability that the market will trade at .6985 rather than .6760, given that the first profit target is half the distance from our entry price compared to where our stop is located. What this means is more often than not, we will hit our first target out of sheer randomness. However, there are two additional reasons why the first target should be hit. As H.M. Gartley mentioned in *Profits in the Stock Market* regarding his namesake pattern, "In eight out of ten cases wherein each of these specific conditions occurs, a rally, which will provide a worthwhile profit, ensues." In other words Gartley is letting us know that his pattern should win more than it loses.

The second reason why we should hit the first target before getting stopped out is the increase of volatility that usually accompanies a retest of a recent high or low. Usually, a market won't rip through significant support or resistance levels without first testing the recent high or low. It is at this moment of uncomfortable indecisiveness that volatility will typically increase before a break or bounce takes place. Therefore, it is very common to hit the first profit target when this type of volatility is displayed at the completion of a TCG786 pattern or a TRG786 pattern.

As expected, we have hit our first target at .6985 in the chart in Figure 6.12. At this level we need to liquidate one of our positions with a 75-point profit. Our net position now is long two contracts. Rather than leaving our stop down at .6760, we need to move it up 50 percent of our initial risk ($150 \times .5 = 75$) or 75 points to .6835. We have now reduced our risk by 83 percent. Our risk on all three contracts initially was 450 points

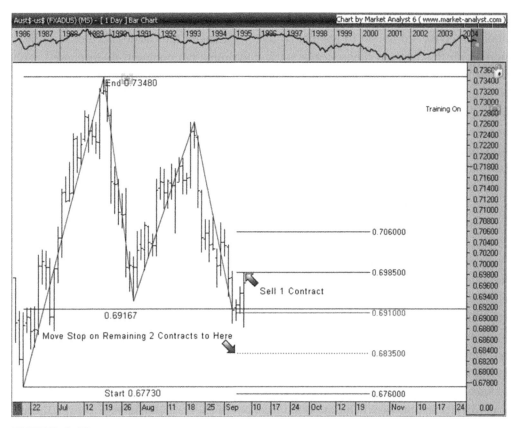

FIGURE 6.12 First Target Hit

(150×3), and now it is only 75 points. This huge 83 percent risk reduction after the first target is hit often confuses some of my students, so let's review how this 83 percent reduction of risk took place.

We've determined that the initial risk on all three contracts was 450 (3×150). Then we took a profit of 75 points when we hit the first target. Now, what is the risk on the remaining two contracts? By moving the stop up 75 points on the two remaining contracts, our risk on each of the contracts becomes 75 points, or a total of 150 point for the two of them. But the risk is not actually 150 points, because we now have to subtract the 75 point profit that we have already made when we liquidated the contract after hitting the first target. When we subtract the 75 point profit from the 150 point risk that we have with the remaining two contracts, this gives us a risk on our overall position of 75 points if we get stopped out at .6835. A 75-point loss is a lot better than a 450-point loss! As discussed previously, hitting our first profit target is a high-probability event.

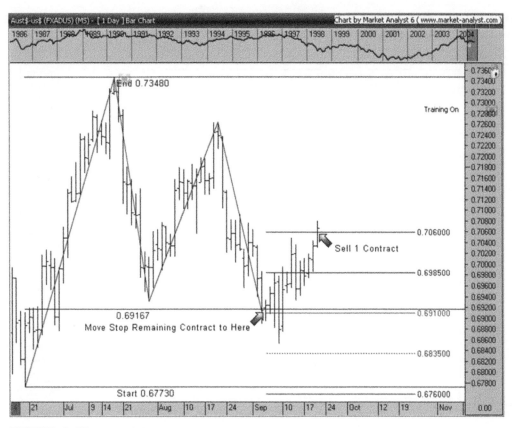

FIGURE 6.13 Second Target Hit

Now that we have hit our "day trader" target at .6985, our focus is on our second profit target at .7060. The second profit target is always 100 percent of our initial risk (150 × 1), or in this case 150 points above our entry price of .6910.

As seen in Figure 6.13, we have hit the second profit target at .7060, and it's time to liquidate our second "swing trader" contract at this level for a 150-point profit. Just as we moved the stop up 75 points when we hit the first profit target, we need to do the same here. Rather than leaving the stop down at .6835, we move it up by 50 percent of our initial risk (150 × .5) or 75 points to .6910, which happens to be the price at which we bought all three contracts. We are now in a very comfortable position. We have locked in a 225-point profit, and our protective stop on the remaining contract is at the same price that we entered. Now we have one contract left, our long-term "position trader" contract. As such, we need to use a big, loose position-trader style of stop on this contract. I refer to this contract as the "lottery ticket" contract, because it doesn't "pay out" as often as the other two contracts do. However, when it does work, you will remind yourself that

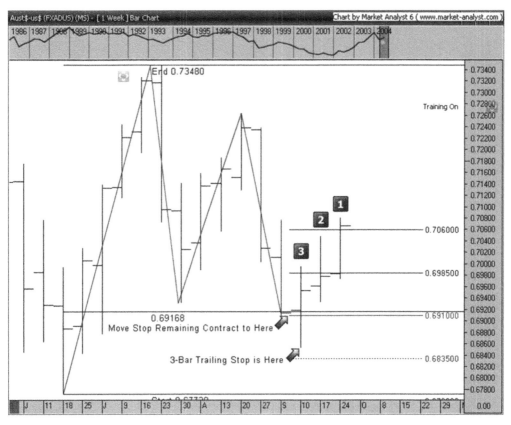

FIGURE 6.14 Changing from Daily to Weekly

the few times in a year that you win the "lottery," it was well worth the time managing your multiple contract positions.

To manage the last position we will use a 3-bar trailing stop, but we are going to use it on the next larger time frame. Our initial trade setup was on the daily chart, so we will use a 3-bar trailing stop on the weekly AUD/USD chart. As shown in Figure 6.14, the Gartley Pattern is still visible, and I have included the profit targets and stop levels for our single in/scale out strategy.

As noted on the chart in Figure 6.14, if we use a 3-bar trailing stop, we have to look back at the last three complete weekly bars on the chart to determine where our stop should be located. The lowest low of the previous three weekly bars is the low of bar number three at .6853. Notice that this low is below our entry price of .6910. That being the case, we will not employ the 3-bar trailing stop on our weekly chart until it exceeds our entry point at .6910. The idea is that we don't want to lose any money on the remaining contract; that means that the 3-bar trailing stop will kick in only when it is above our entry point. Figure 6.15 shows when the 3-bar trailing stop begins to take effect.

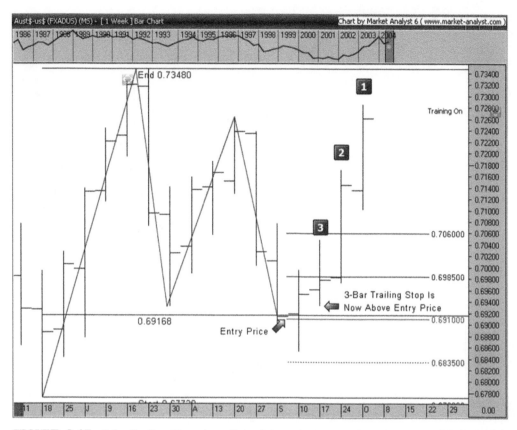

FIGURE 6.15 3-Bar Trailing Stop above Entry Price

In Figure 6.15 we can see that the 3-bar trailing stop on bar number three is now above the entry price of .6910. The 3-bar trailing stop kicks in on the weekly chart, and we now have our "lottery ticket." The result appears in Figure 6.16.

The line shown under the bars in Figure 6.16 is an automatic 3-bar trailing stop available in Market Analyst. The 3-bar trailing stop on the weekly AUD/USD would have kept us in the trade for more than three months until we took off our last position at .7680.

To review, we had an initial risk of 450 points. Hitting the first target paid us 75 points and reduced our risk to 75 points or 83 percent. The second target paid us 150 points, and our stop was moved to entry, thus theoretically eliminating the chance that our profit would turn into a loss. The last position or "lottery ticket" was liquidated for a 770 point profit. The single in/scale out strategy works well in all markets and all time frames. Even if you choose not to trade Gartley Patterns, do yourself a favor and start using the single in/scale out trade management strategy with your existing trade setups; you will be glad you did!

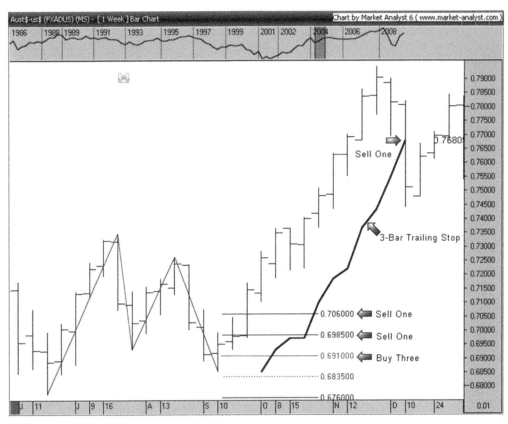

FIGURE 6.16 Result of Single In/Scale Out Strategy

Scale In/Single Out

As mentioned, an alternative method of managing your trade is with a martingale-style money management system. I refer to this strategy as scale in/single out. As stated previously, this method of money management is very aggressive, but it will allow you to "turn a loser into a winner" in the majority of cases.

Gamblers are familiar with the "doubling-down" concept, and it can be applied to trading as well. If you like the idea of being "right" most of the time, this strategy will appeal to you. However, there is a price to be paid for the luxury of being "right" most of the time. When you are wrong, you are really wrong!

To apply a scale in/single out method of trade management, we have to create a "scale," or an interval for our chart. To determine the right scale, we must look over the previous history of the instrument in question to determine the optimal value of the scale. Once this has been determined, we are ready to trade.

For example, let's imagine that you want to trade a bullish TCG786 on the EUR/USD and the EUR/USD is currently at 1.4000. You determine that the optimal scale for the EUR/USD is 100 pips. You enter the trade with a single contract at 1.4000, with a profit target at 1.4100. If the EUR/USD goes up to 1.4100, then you have made 100 points and the TCG786 worked and you would have a 100 point profit. But what happens if the EUR/USD goes down? The idea is that we want to double our position size at each 100-point interval. If the EUR/USD drops to 1.3900, we would buy two more contracts (double our previous quantity purchased) and change our target from 1.4100 to 1.4000. If the EUR/USD rallies to 1.4000, then we would break even on the first contract that we bought at 1.4000, and we would make 200 points on the two contracts that we purchased at 1.3900. If the EUR/USD continued to decline to 1.3800, then we would buy four more contracts (double our previous purchase quantity) and change our profit target from 1.4000 to 1.3900, and so on.

If you haven't heard of this before, don't get too excited about this idea. There are definite disadvantages to using a martingale trade management system. The first issue is that it requires a significant amount of capital. In theory, this money management method is bulletproof except for one small issue—money. Do you have unlimited capital to weather a big drawdown in your account if necessary? The other disadvantage with martingales is the risk of ruin. You *must* have a limit on how many intervals that you will go to; otherwise, it is a matter of time before you switch back to the single in/scale out strategy or before you will quit trading altogether. I always put a stop at the fourth interval. Therefore, when I get stopped, it is at a big loss on seven contracts. The good part about the strategy is that you have a high percent chance of winning. Make sure you have specific rules in place before you initiate a position with this strategy. Don't fool yourself into thinking that your system won't break because of historical stats; stuff happens!

Let's look at an example of a cotton trade signal. The signal was to sell cotton at 57.00. In the chart in Figure 6.17, we have applied the single in/scale out targets. You can see that we would have been filled on three contracts at 57.00, liquidated one position at 54.50, and then stopped out on the remaining two contracts at 59.50 for a loss.

Now let's see what happened when we applied the scale in/single out strategy to the same trade. As seen in Figure 6.18, we would have sold one contract at 57.00 with our profit target at 52.00. Cotton dipped temporarily but then rallied up to our next interval at 62.00. At 62.00, we sold two more contracts so that our next position was short three contracts. The next interval to sell would have been up at 67.00; however, cotton weakened before it went up further. When we were filled at 62.00, we moved our profit target higher from 52.00 up to 57.00. About a week after we added to our position at 62.00, cotton dropped to 57.00 and we would have liquidated our positions for a profit.

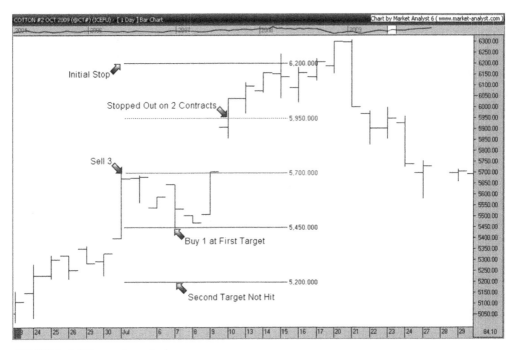

FIGURE 6.17   Single In/Scale Out

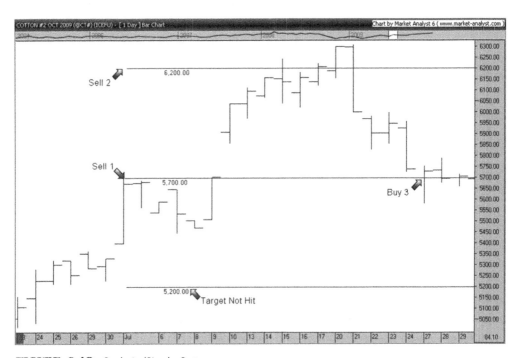

FIGURE 6.18   Scale In/Single Out

As you can see from our cotton examples in Figures 6.17 and 6.18, the single in/scale out strategy ended with a loss, whereas the scale in/single out strategy would have ended with a profit.

In Chapter 6, we have examined the elements of different trade entry and exit signals. In addition, we have explored the option of entering the market with multiple contracts by scaling in or scaling out of a position. In Chapter 7 we examine real-world situations with case studies that apply everything we have learned up to this point.

Case Studies

Now that we've covered some of the strategies for entry and exit, let's look at some case studies. The following four case studies will reinforce what you've learned in the previous chapters and show you how to use that information to make a trading decision. These are real trade setups that I published in advance in the *Gartley Trader Futures and Forex Report* in 2009.

CASE STUDY NO. 1

The first case study focuses on a trade signal published in the *Gartley Trader Futures Report* from the week of October 19, 2009. The setup is illustrated in Figure 7.1 and is shown in the 60-minute continuous sugar (ICE) chart. From early September (indicated by the W) sugar continued to rise up to point X on October 1. We have applied a 3 percent swing chart overlay to identify the significant corrections that took place during this rally.

In regard to volume, remember Gartley's statement regarding this phase: "activity has shown a definite tendency to dry up, indication that liquidation is terminating." Notice the volume window displayed under the chart; a trendline has been plotted to indicate the reduction of volume on sugar during this initial W–X phase.

Let's now focus our attention on the X–A leg in Figure 7.1. Notably, the swing plotted from the 3 percent swing chart overlay shows us that the X–A leg is greater in price and time compared with the other bearish swings displayed. This indicates that a potential high is in place at point X, and there could be a fundamental change of trend taking place. Elliott wave obsessives will notice a textbook 5-wave sequence during the X–A leg. Is this mandatory? No, but a five-wave subdivision is a very common occurrence

FIGURE 7.1 Volume for W-X and X-A

during the X–A leg. In addition, look at the increase in volume taking place during the X–A leg as indicated by the trendline drawn in the volume window. Gartley stated that he wanted to see "volume expanding on the upside" in regard to the X–A leg.

We have yet to see an AB = CD in the recent rally, but we still have enough data points to plot our price retracement and price extension. Notice the decline in volume in respect to the A–D rally. Remember that this was an important aspect of Gartley's "One of the Best Trading Opportunities."

Now we need to apply a price-extension tool to identify where the D point should be. In Figure 7.2, we have applied the quadrilateral to identify where the potential D point of AB = CD in price and time at the tip of the quadrilateral.

The next tool we will use is the price-retracement tool. As shown in Figure 7.3, the tip of the quadrilateral is landing right beside the 78.6 percent retracement at 24.47. Due to the proximity of the horizontal Fibonacci retracement line and the tip of the quadrilateral, the expectation is that a trend reversal is due.

Now we have to make a decision regarding our entry technique. In this example I use the single in/scale out method of money management. The *Gartley Trader Futures Report* from that week says, "We have a potential bearish Gartley pattern on the 60 minute continuous SB chart. If SB rallies to 24.50 before it trades below 22.51, the bearish Gartley pattern should be complete and we will want to enter with limit orders on the short side."

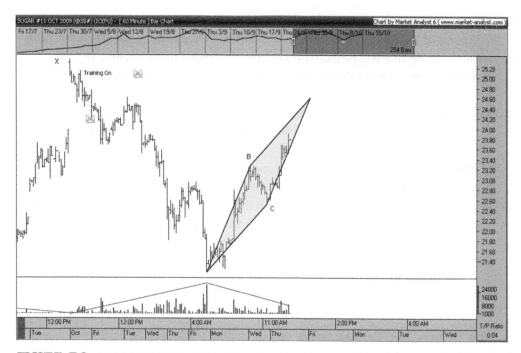

FIGURE 7.2 Quadrilateral Price Extension

FIGURE 7.3 Quadrilateral Clustering with 78.6 Percent

Why do we use 22.51 as a place where our trade will be invalid? If sugar breaks the low of the C point of the pattern, then the AB = CD would have to be recalculated, because the more recent decline will be more pronounced compared to the existing B–C leg.

The trade management rules are spelled out for us in the report as follows:

Entry order. Sell three contracts at 24.50 with limit orders. Enter the protective buy stop on all three contracts at 25.50. Set the first profit target to buy one contract on a limit at 24.00.

If the first target is hit. Move the protective buy stop on the remaining two contracts to 25.00 and set the second profit target to buy one contract at 23.50.

If second target is hit. Move the stop on the remaining open position to 24.50 and use a 3-bar trailing stop on the daily chart as long as the 3-bar trailing stop is below 24.50.

3-Bar trailing stop. The 3-bar trailing stop in the preceding example would put a stop above the highest high of the previous three bars (ignoring inside bars) on a daily chart.

Now we need to enter limit orders on our trading platform; sell three contracts at 24.50 limit. If we get filled on the order, we will need to put our stops above the X point at 25.50. Let's add some more bars to the chart to see whether we get filled.

In Figure 7.4 we can see that sugar hit 24.50 and did not trade below 22.51 so as to invalidate the trade. Now we sell three contracts at 24.50. Next, we have to set our profit targets. Using the single in/scale out levels tool in Market Analyst, we click the level where we sold our three contracts at 24.50 and click the 25.50 level where our stops are. The software automatically calculates our targets and stops according to the single in/scale out method, as shown in Figure 7.5.

Now that we are filled, we have to enter an order for a protective stop; buy three contracts on a stop at 25.50. This level is identified for us in Figure 7.6.

In addition to the stop, we need to enter another order for our first profit target; buy one contract on a limit at 24.00. The worst-case scenario now is that sugar might rally up to 25.50 and stop us out on all three contracts. However, this rarely happens; we know that the first profit target is twice as close to our entry price than where our stop is. Therefore, hitting the first profit target is a much more probable event than getting stopped out. Let's see if this is the case in our situation.

As shown in the chart in Figure 7.7, we hit the first profit target at 24.00, and we buy back one sugar contract on a limit and we move our stop to 25.00. Therefore, we cancel the order to buy two contracts at 25.50 on a stop, and we enter a new order to buy two contracts at 25.00 on a stop. At this point it is possible for us still to lose money on this trade; however, even if we get stopped out now on the two remaining contracts at 25.00, we have reduced our risk by 83 percent.

FIGURE 7.4 Filled with the 78.6 Percent Fib Entry Method

FIGURE 7.5 Profit and Stop Levels Set

FIGURE 7.6 Stop and First Target Entered

FIGURE 7.7 First Target Hit

FIGURE 7.8 Second Target Hit

We are now hoping that sugar will drop and hit our next profit target, so we enter a new order to buy one contract at 23.50 on a limit. Let's see what happens.

As shown in Figure 7.8, our order was filled and we buy back our second contract at 23.50. We are still short one contract, so we have to cancel the open order to buy two contracts on a stop at 25.00 and enter a new order to buy one contract on a stop at 24.50. Our stop on the remaining contract is at our entry point, so even if we get stopped out at 24.50, the trade will still be profitable. Some people call this last contract a "free trade," or "using the house's money"; I just call it the "lottery ticket" contract.

As discussed previously, at this point we want to change time frames. Why? From experience, if you stay on the same time frame, the single in/scale out method still works fine; however, the last contract doesn't seem to participate in the big position trader moves unless the time frame is changed. Remember, we looked at the difference between a 3-bar trailing stop on a daily and a weekly chart in Figures 6.9 and 6.10. The difference in profits can be substantial when the time frame is changed. We were advised in the *Gartley Trader Futures Report* to use a 3-bar trailing stop on the daily chart. We will now change the chart from 60 minutes to daily, as shown in Figure 7.9.

In Figure 7.9, the single in/scale out levels that we added to the 60-minute chart are still visible. Notice the daily bar that hit our second target at 23.50? This is the day when our 3-bar trailing stop kicks in. The automatic 3-bar trailing stop in Market Analyst is

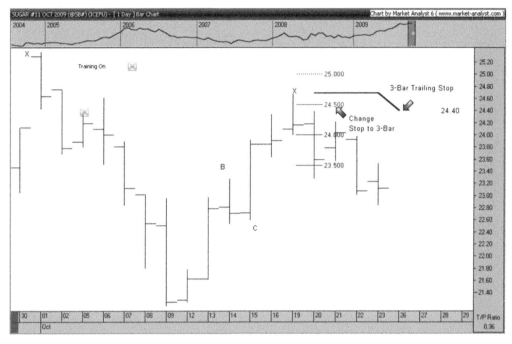

FIGURE 7.9 Daily Chart with 3-Bar Trailing Stop

displayed for us, but notice that the stop line is above the entry price at 24.50. Where should our stop be? Remember, as discussed previously, when we get to the last open contract of the three that we put on, we do not want to lose anything on the last contract. For that reason, the minimum place for our stop would be at 24.50 and no higher. It is not until the 3-bar trailing stop line dips below the 24.50 level that the 3-bar trailing stop kicks in. In Figure 7.9, this event occurs at the last bar on the right, where the 3-bar trailing stop is now set to 24.40. Now that the 3-bar trailing stop has kicked in, we will have to occasionally adjust our stop. As we will be calculating the 3-bar trailing stop on the daily chart, we will have to look at our at chart once a day at the end of the trading session to see whether we need to replace our existing stop order with a different price.

Let's add some more bars to our sugar trade to see the final result.

In Figure 7.10, we were finally stopped out on the daily chart with our 3-bar trailing stop at 22.91. The results of our bearish TRG786 example for sugar from the *Gartley Trader Futures Report* are as follows:

- Sold one contract at 24.50, bought one at 24.00.
- Sold one contract at 24.50, bought one at 23.50.
- Sold one contract at 24.50, bought one at 22.91.
- Profit = 3.09 × $1,120 = $3,460.80.

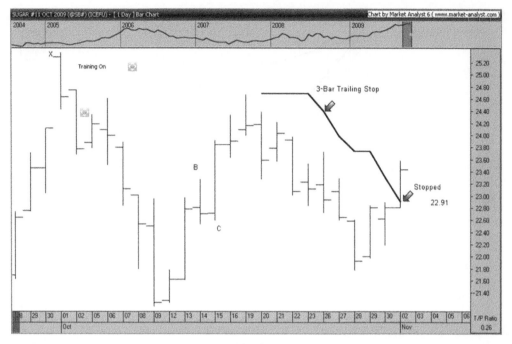

FIGURE 7.10 Stopped Out with 3-Bar Trailing Stop

Overall, this was a nice example of a TRG786 trade using the single in/scale out method of money management. Let's consider another example, but this time it will be a TCG. Remember, with trend continuation Gartleys, we won't be looking at volume.

CASE STUDY NO. 2

The next example is a trade signal published in the *Gartley Trader Futures Report* for the week of December 7, 2009. The setup, illustrated in Figure 7.11, is the 360-minute continuous crude oil (NYMEX) chart.

From late September to late October, crude continued to rise. This would be the X–A leg of our trend-continuation Gartley, given that the price action before the September low looks corrective in nature; therefore, we are not looking for a trend reversal but for a trend continuation. Once again this X–A leg looks like a 5-wave Elliott Wave sequence, but it doesn't matter; we are simply looking for something that resembles a trend.

Following the X–A trend move, can you discern an ABC Elliott Wave correction or an AB = CD? We have applied the quadrilateral as our price-extension tool to identify where the end of this correction should terminate.

FIGURE 7.11 Potential Bullish TCG786 in Crude

The next tool we will need to use is the price-retracement tool. As you can see in Figure 7.11, the tip of the quadrilateral is landing closer to the 78.6 percent Fibonacci retracement than to the 61.8 percent Fibonacci retracement. Therefore, we expect to see the completion of a TCG786 shortly.

Once again, we will use the single in/scale out method of money management. The *Gartley Trader Futures Report* said,

> We have a potential bullish Gartley pattern on the 360 minute continuous CL chart. If CL declines to 70 before it trades above 78.90, the bullish Gartley pattern should be complete and we will want to enter with limit orders on the long side. Depending on your account size you may choose to use mini contacts or an at the money option at the entry price. If the option doubles in price, liquidate.

The 78.90 level is identified as the point where the trade would be invalid, and on page 5 of the report we find trade management rules for the single in/scale out strategy, which are listed as follows:

- **Entry order.** Buy three contracts at 70.00 with limit orders. Enter the protective sell stop on all three contracts at 65.00. Set the first profit target to sell one contract on a limit at 72.50.

- **If the first target is hit.** Move the protective sell stop on the remaining two contracts to 67.50 and set the second profit target to sell one contract at 75.00.
- **If the second target is hit.** Move the stop on the remaining open position to 70.00 and use a 3-bar trailing stop on the daily chart as long as the 3-bar trailing stop is above 70.00.
- **3-Bar trailing stop.** The 3-bar trailing stop in the preceding example would put a stop below the lowest low of the previous three bars (ignoring inside bars) on a daily chart.

Using Market Analyst's single in/scale out tool, we click the entry price ($70.00) and the stop price ($65.00) to display the levels for us automatically, as shown in Figure 7.12.

Now we need to enter limit orders; buy three contracts at 70.00 limit. If we get filled on the order, we will put our stops on all three contracts below the late September low (X point) at 65.00. Let's add some more bars to the chart to see whether we get filled.

In Figure 7.13 we can see that crude hit 70.00 and did not trade above 78.90 so as to invalidate the trade. Now that we have bought three contracts at 70.00, we have to set our stops; sell three contracts on a stop at 65.00. This level is identified for us in

FIGURE 7.12 Profit Targets and Stops Set

FIGURE 7.13 Orders Filled at $70.00

Figure 7.13. In addition to the stop, we need to enter another order for our first profit target; sell one contract limit at 72.50. Let's see what happens next.

As shown in Figure 7.14, we have hit our first profit target at 72.50, and we sell one contract on a limit. We now have to replace our order to sell three contracts on a stop at 65.00 with one to sell two contracts on a stop at 67.50. Once again we have reduced our risk by 83 percent. We also have to place an order for our second target at 75.00; sell one contract at 75.00 limit. We are now hoping that crude will rally and hit our next profit target. Let's see what happens.

As shown in Figure 7.15, our order was filled, and we sold a second contract at 75.00. We are still long one contract, and so we need to cancel the open order to sell two contracts on a stop at 67.50. We now put a protective stop in on the last contract at our entry price; sell one contract on a stop at 70.00. At this point, even if we get stopped out, we would still be profitable.

Do you remember what we have to do next? We were advised in the *Gartley Trader Futures Report* to use a 3-bar trailing stop on the daily chart. So we now have to change from a 360-minute chart to a daily chart. As long as the automatic 3-bar trailing stop line is above the 70.00, we will use it. Let's add the automatic 3-bar trailing stop on the daily chart to see the final result.

FIGURE 7.14 First Target Hit

FIGURE 7.15 Second Target Hit

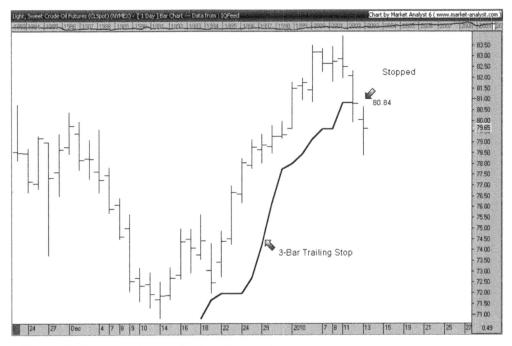

FIGURE 7.16   Stopped Out with a 3-Bar Trailing Stop

In Figure 7.16, we were finally stopped out on the daily chart with our 3-bar trailing stop at 80.83. The results of our bearish TRG786 example for sugar from the *Gartley Trader Futures Report* were as follows:

- Bought one contract at 70.00, sold one at 72.50.
- Bought one contract at 70.00, sold one at 75.00.
- Bought one contract at 70.00, sold one at 80.83.
- Profit = $18.33 × $1,000 = $18,330.

This is a nice example of a TCG786 trade using the single in/scale out method with crude oil futures. You might be thinking that you would never trade three regular-size crude contracts with a five-dollar stop. The *Gartley Trader Futures Report* is for beginners and professionals. I have a subscriber on the floor of the NYMEX who uses the signals on regular sized contracts because he has the available capital to trade this way. If you don't have the capital, that's OK; just don't take the trade or look for smaller contracts. For an example, we discussed the regular CL 1,000-barrel crude contract. You could also trade other products such as the miNY crude contract, which is 500 barrels. Or you could trade oil stocks, an ETF, a narrow-based index, an option, and so forth. The *Gartley Trader Futures Report* gives signals; it's up to you how you wish to execute those signals if you don't have enough capital in your account.

Another concern someone might have about the trade is that the risk-to-reward ratio ended up getting close to 1:1. Is 1:1 really a concern? Consider this: If you were betting on heads or tails and you knew that the coin you were flipping was weighted toward the tails side, would you be interested in making a bet? In addition, if you decided to bet even money, how many flips would you like to commit to? One? One hundred? One thousand? Hopefully you get the point.

The Gartley isn't perfect, and so to keep things in perspective, let's look at a trade where we had a loss.

CASE STUDY NO. 3

The next TCG example is a signal published in the *Gartley Trader Forex Report* for the week of June 22, 2009. The chart in Figure 7.17 is the daily chart of the EUR/USD (SPOT). Can you see a Gartley Pattern?

It appears that there may be a bearish TCG pattern in the EUR/USD. To make sure, we have to apply the price-retracement and quadrilateral tools to the chart. From December 2008 to March 2009, there appeared to be an impulsive trend move to the downside. This would be the X–A leg of our trend continuation. Following the X–A trend move, there was an ABC Elliott Wave correction or an AB = CD. We have applied the

FIGURE 7.17 Daily EUR/USD

FIGURE 7.18 Quadrilateral Applied

quadrilateral as our price extension tool to identify the time and price target where the countertrend should terminate. This is illustrated for us in Figure 7.18.

After applying the quadrilateral tool to the corrective portion of our chart, we now calculate a 78.6 percent Fibonacci retracement on the X–A leg. This retracement level is 1.4214 and is displayed in the chart in Figure 7.19.

As we can see, the tip of the quadrilateral is just beyond the 78.6 percent Fibonacci retracement. Due to the proximity of these two tools, we have confirmed that we have the completion of a TCG786 pattern. However, the issue with this setup is that it has already happened. The *Gartley Trader Forex Report* comes out once a week on Monday, and on June 22, 2009 the EUR/USD had already weakened a bit. So what should we do?

It will happen from time to time that you will spot a Gartley that has already completed. When this happens, simply ask, "Does the pattern still appear valid? Has the market had a significant reversal in the area of my cluster?" If the pattern still appears to be valid and the market hasn't experienced a significant change of sentiment, then simply put limit orders in to get filled in the area that the pattern completed. This typically is the Fibonacci level where the pattern completes; however, it could be at another level. The reason that we cannot be dogmatic about this is because sometimes there can be another "mini-Gartley" on a shorter time frame from the one we are trading off of, and we may choose to use that setup rather than the previous one.

FIGURE 7.19 78.6 Percent Fibonacci Retracement Applied

In this example, the *Gartley Trader Forex Report* states, "We have a bearish Gartley setting up in the EUR/USD on the daily chart. The pattern is based on a 78.6 percent Fibonacci retracement and a simple ABC zigzag that completes at 1.4165. If the EUR/USD rallies this week to 1.4215 before it goes below 1.3749, the bearish Gartley pattern will be complete and we will want to enter with limit orders on the short side."

The orders are spelled out for us in the newsletter as follows:

- **Entry order.** Sell three contracts at 1.4215 with limit orders. Enter the protective buy stop on all three contracts at 1.4355. Set the first profit target to buy one contract on a limit at 1.4145.
- **If the first target is hit.** Move the protective buy stop on the remaining two contracts to 1.4285 and set the second profit target to buy one contract at 1.4065.
- **If the second target is hit.** Move the stop on the remaining open position to 1.4215 and use a 3-bar trailing stop on the weekly chart as long as the 3-bar trailing stop is below 1.4215.
- **3-Bar trailing stop.** The 3-bar trailing stop in the preceding example would put a stop above the highest high of the previous three bars (ignoring inside bars) on a weekly chart.

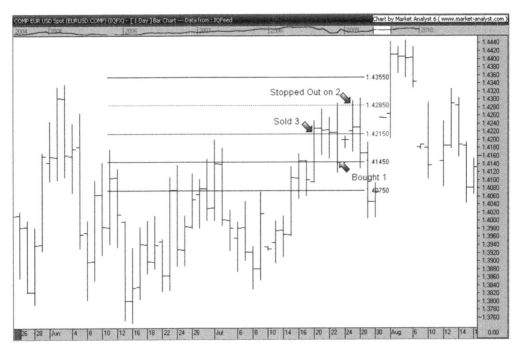

FIGURE 7.20   Stopped Out

The result of this trade is shown in Figure 7.20.

In Figure 7.20, we can see where we were filled on our initial order of selling three contracts at 1.4215. Three days later we hit our first profit target at 1.4145. At that point we would have canceled our stops on three contracts at 1.4355 and put in a new stop order on two contracts at 1.4285. Two days later, the EUR/USD rallied, and we were stopped out at 1.4285. The results of our bearish TRG786 example for the EUR/USD from the *Gartley Trader* newsletter were as follows:

- Sold one contract at 1.4215, bought one at 1.4145.
- Sold one contract at 1.4215, bought one at 1.4285.
- Sold one contract at 1.4215, bought one at 1.4285.
- Loss = 70 Points × $10.00 = ($700).

The potential risk on this trade was initially 420 points for a potential $4,200 loss. However, we got away with a $700 loss. In my opinion, getting into a position to trade a big Gartley off a daily chart and losing only $700 is a "win."

Once again, if the foregoing numbers make you nervous, don't trade the big contracts. Many spot Forex dealers offer mini contracts and micro-mini contracts in Forex.

Let's look at one more example.

CASE STUDY NO. 4

Our last example is a bullish TRG786 pattern. This signal was published in the *Gartley Trader Futures Report* for the week of March 9, 2009. The setup is illustrated in Figure 7.21 and is the daily continuous wheat (CBOT) chart. From the high in March 2008 (indicated by the W), wheat declined down to the low made at point X in December 2008.

Remember with the TRG patterns, we are looking for Gartley's volume rules for the W–X leg. Gartley stated that "activity has shown a definite tendency to dry up, indication that liquidation is terminating." Notice the volume window displayed under the chart; a trendline has been plotted to indicate the reduction of volume on wheat during this initial W–X phase.

Now let's now focus our attention on the X–A leg in Figure 7.21. It appears that the X–A leg could be indicating a reversal in trend. The X–A leg is greater in price and time compared to previous swings in the same direction since the summer. This indicates that a potential low could be in place at point X. In addition, look at the increase in volume taking place during the X–A leg, as indicated by the trendline drawn in the volume window. Gartley stated that he wanted to see "volume expanding on the upside" in regard to the X–A leg.

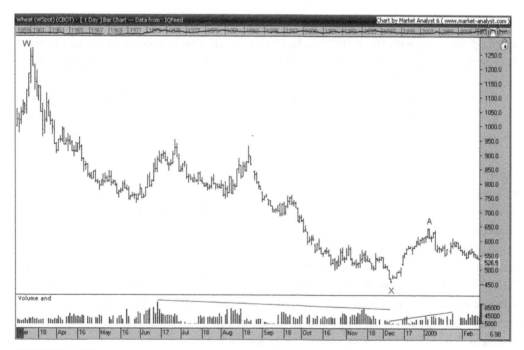

FIGURE 7.21 W–X Volume Decline, X–A Volume Increase

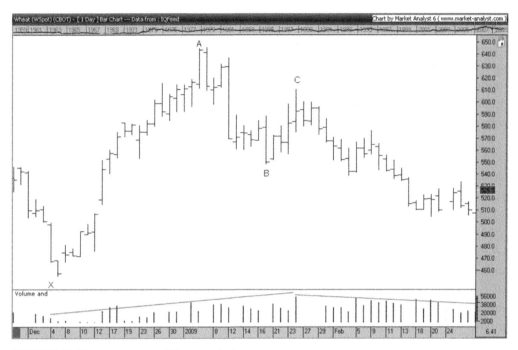

FIGURE 7.22   Decrease in Volume on A–D

Now let's zoom in to see rest of the pattern. As we can see in Figure 7.22, we have supplied the chart with the XABC labels. Notice the decline in volume in respect to the A–D decline as indicated by the trendline in the volume window. Remember that this was an important aspect of Gartley's rule on volume.

Now we need to apply a price-extension tool to identify where the D point should be. In Figure 7.23 we have applied the quadrilateral to identify the D point of AB = CD in price and time.

The next tool we will need to use is the price retracement tool. As is apparent in Figure 7.24, the quadrilateral is landing right beside the 78.6 percent retracement. This means that there is a higher probability that there will be a trend reversal at the 78.6 percent level instead of at the other Fibonacci levels, resulting from the proximity of the quadrilateral tip to the 78.6 percent level.

In Figure 7.24, the tip of the quadrilateral is just above the 78.6 percent Fibonacci retracement at 495.9. We have now confirmed that we have the completion of a bullish TRG786 pattern in wheat. What method of money management will we use? My favorite is the single in/scale out method. Let's use the single in/scale out levels in Market Analyst. Our levels are automatically displayed on the chart with two clicks, one click at the entry level and one click at the initial stop level, as shown in Figure 7.25.

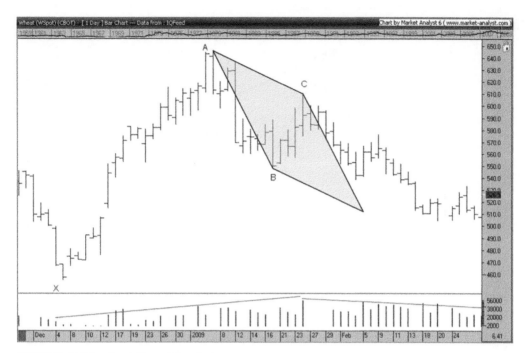

FIGURE 7.23 Quadrilateral Applied

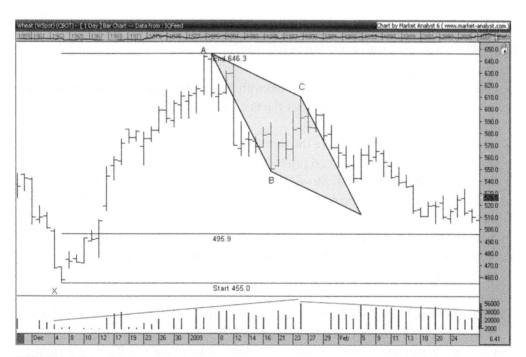

FIGURE 7.24 78.6 Percent Retracement

FIGURE 7.25 Profit and Stop Levels

So now it's time to place our orders on the broker platform. According to the *Gartley Trader Futures Report*, the orders are as follows:

- **Entry order.** Buy three contracts at 496 with limit orders. Enter the protective sell stop on all three contracts at 451. Set the first profit target to sell one contract on a limit at 518.5.
- **If the first target is hit.** Move the protective sell stop on the remaining two contracts to 473.5 and set the second profit target to sell one contract at 541.
- **If the second target is hit.** Move the stop on the remaining open position to 496 and use a 3-bar trailing stop on the weekly chart as long as the 3-bar trailing stop is above 496.
- **3-Bar trailing stop.** The 3-bar trailing stop in the preceding example would put a stop below the highest high of the previous three bars (ignoring inside bars) on a weekly chart.

Let's add some bars to see if we get filled on our order to buy three contracts at 496.

In Figure 7.26 we can see that wheat dropped to 496. Now we have bought three contracts at 496 and placed a protective stop on all three contracts at 451. We have included

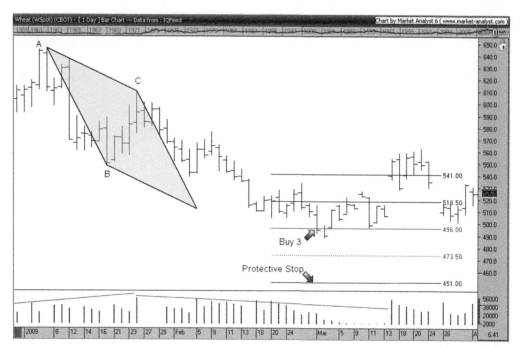

FIGURE 7.26 Buy Three Contracts, Enter Stops

some future bars on the chart to give you a different perspective and so that you can compare Figure 7.26 with Figures 7.27 and 7.28.

In Figure 7.27, we hit our first target at 518.5 and moved our stop up to 473.5.

In Figure 7.28, we hit our second target at 541 and moved our stop up to 496. Remember what we need to do now? Switch time frames for the "lottery ticket" trade. We are changing our view from the daily to the weekly chart of wheat. Then we apply the 3-bar trailing stop on the weekly as long as the stop remains above 496.

As shown in Figure 7.29, we changed our time frame to weekly and applied the 3-bar trailing stop. The 3-bar trailing stop took us out of our last contract at 576. Remember, managing a 3-bar trailing stop on a weekly chart means that you only have to look at your chart once a week to see whether the stop needs to be adjusted. The results of our bullish TRG786 example for CBOT wheat are as follows:

- Bought one contract at 496, sold one at 518.5.
- Bought one contract at 496, sold one at 541.
- Bought one contract at 496, sold one at 576.
- Profit = 147.5 points × $10.00 = $7,375.

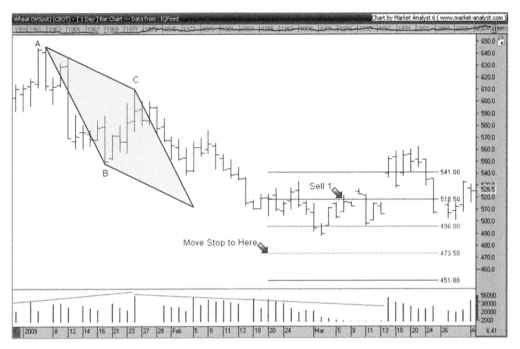

FIGURE 7.27 First Target Hit, Move Stop

FIGURE 7.28 Second Target Hit, Move Stop

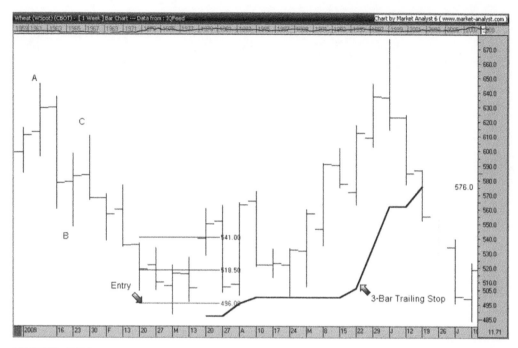

FIGURE 7.29 3-Bar Trailing Stop on Weekly Chart

In Chapter 7, we have considered four real-world examples of how to trade TRGs and TCGs using the single in/scale out trade management strategy. You now know enough to be dangerous. But before you run out and put on some trades with your newfound knowledge, it is essential that you read Chapter 8 to learn how to develop your personal trading plan and a trading journal.

Plans and Journals

My friend Robert Miner wrote a book entitled *Dynamic Trading*. The idea behind the word "dynamic" is an important concept in understanding how to achieve trading nirvana. The word "dynamic" comes from Greek and can be translated simply as "related to power." A further definition of dynamic is "of or relating to energy or to objects in motion; characterized by continuous change, activity, or progress." Given this definition, we would all agree that the financial markets are dynamic in the sense that the energy or power of individuals is responsible for the market's continuous change. Therefore, there is *one* thing that we know with certainty about the financial markets—they constantly change. They are not based on static, perfect, fixed-length cycles that continue to repeat forever. This is an important concept, because it has a bearing on what we should do with our positions if the market starts to move against us.

As we have discussed, the Gartley Pattern setup is only one part of the trading puzzle. Once a position has been taken and new information becomes available, you might need to make a new decision based on new information instead of sticking with the old decision based on old information. Guys might stereotype girls and complain about how girls keep changing their minds. Or are the girls simply trying to make better decisions by considering the most current information? The ancient Persian kings had a rule that once the king established a law, it couldn't be changed, not even by the king himself! Guys, are we like that? Our egos get in the way, don't they? Start listening to the GPS when you get lost in the car. You might even consider something incredibly difficult if you are a married man—listening to your wife!

Let's imagine that you wanted to take your family on a picnic. You have one week to plan the food, drinks, activities, and all the other details to make sure that it's the best picnic ever. The day before the picnic, the weather forecast states that there is a

98 percent chance of precipitation. Based on the time you spent planning for the picnic, would you still insist that everyone in your family attend, because there is a 2 percent chance that it *won't* rain? Would you conclude that you are a bad father because you didn't take your family on a picnic; that you aren't a "man" because you are changing your mind?

This illustration may seem ridiculous, but do you see the parallels with trading? Despite all the mental energy that we put into our analyses, sometimes we will be wrong. New information is being made available to you every second. Does the new information confirm what you believed, or does it tell you that you might be wrong? Holding on to a position that appears to have a 98 percent chance of losing is about as smart as the father's forcing his family to go to a picnic in the rain. The family will respect the father for his flexibility in not forcing them to go to a picnic in the rain; similarly, traders are rewarded for flexibility when it comes to acting on new information.

DEVELOPING A TRADING PLAN

So as you are about to consider developing your trading plan, how can you be dynamic or flexible and yet have a solid trading plan that you can adhere to?

The easy part of writing your trading plan is establishing rules for the setup. The difficult part is how you will manage the trade once you've entered the market. Within the plan, you should identify various market conditions that could take place *after* you initiate a trade. At least five types of scenario can take place after you put on a position:

1. Strongly bullish.
2. Moderately bullish.
3. Neutral.
4. Moderately bearish.
5. Strongly bearish.

Your trading plan must be flexible enough to accommodate, at a minimum, these five variables. It is impossible to list all future financial events in a trading plan, but we should have these five situations listed at minimum.

You will notice in the trading plan sample found in the following section that I do not list five different exit strategies based on the foregoing five scenarios. The reason for this is that the trading plan uses the single in/scale out method of trade management, which was discussed previously. In my opinion, the single in/scale out method covers the listed five scenarios. It allows us to have rules in place, but it also allows us to make adjustments to our trading practice based on new, future information. The list of possible scenarios is for the individual who wishes to use a technique other than the single in/scale out method, while allowing for flexibility within the framework of his or her trading plan.

Remember that most "new" information is being digested by the markets very quickly to reflect it. Therefore, the only "new" information that we should focus on is the price action on the charts, not a "talking head" on TV discussing things that have already happened.

One of the five listed categories is more important than the rest. Do you know which one? It is category number one if you are short (and category number five if you are long). Having a stop in place when you are dead wrong is the most important stop of all. Some have decided at some point in their trading careers (including myself) not to put in a stop and to say "we'll see how it goes." Should we allow for this type of "dynamic trading?"

A construction worker may conclude that he doesn't need to wear a hard hat because he has never been hit in the head—in fact, he's never seen anyone hit in the head on a construction site. As we all know, if he doesn't wear the hard hat, it takes only one mistake and his construction career will be over. It's similar with trading. We must be prepared for the worst possible scenarios, even if they have never happened before. We place orders in the market to protect ourselves from a potential trading catastrophe in the same way that a construction worker wears a hard hat. I don't think there are many construction workers who enjoy wearing a hard hat; it's about as gratifying as putting stop loss orders in the market. However, protective stops and hard hats save careers and lives.

With this in mind, it's important to define exactly where the stops should be and to have crystal clear rules as to how you are going to adjust them before you place a trade. These rules must be written down in a trading plan.

After getting this far in the book, you might be excited to get out there and find some TRG786s. But isn't it true that you've found out about other exciting trade setups in the past? Why aren't you still excited about them? The typical response is, "They didn't work." From a professional trader's point of view, this answer is not acceptable. "Why didn't they work?" is a better question. How many times didn't they work? How many times did they work? What were the rules? Did you change the rules? Did you have enough money?

If it is your intention just to give it a shot with the Gartley Pattern, please don't take that approach. I would appreciate it if you abstain from forming an opinion about the method if you don't have enough results to form an opinion. If you treat trading the Gartley as a "hobby," it will pay you like a hobby. On the other hand, if you are excited and serious about this, then before you put a trade on, you *must* create a written trading plan.

One of the first and most crucial points that should be in a trader's trading plan or business plan is how much to risk on any one trade. If you don't define your risk on a trade, you are potentially risking everything in your account. Defining our personal risk tolerance is Trading 101. Will you risk 5 percent of your existing capital on any one trade? Or 3 percent? Or 1 percent? There is no incorrect answer to this question except, "I don't know how much money I am risking on this trade." To define your personal risk tolerance on any single trade, try the following exercise. Imagine that you have saved up $10,000 over a few years to trade with. Now imagine that you execute a trade according to the instructions in your trading plan and you lose $500. You now have $9,500 in your trading account. How do you feel? Do you feel that the $500 was too much money to lose on the trade? What number would make you feel better? $300? $100? There is no correct answer to this question. Whatever number you choose is the percentage you should risk on any one trade.

I find that most people don't have the discipline to write out a trading plan. Why is it that people will get anal about writing out a business plan if they are going to open a small business with start-up capital of $10,000 or $20,000, but these same people will open a trading account with $50,000 and never get around to writing a trading plan? Do professional traders document their method of trading in a written trading plan? Do professional traders compile the results of all their trades? Of course they do, and if you want to be a professional trader, I would suggest that you start these habits sooner rather than later.

SAMPLE TRADING PLAN

What follows is a model of a trading plan that can be used as a template. Feel free to modify it according to your own needs. I know some will still refuse to write out a trading plan, despite my reminding them that if they "fail to plan, plan to fail." If this applies to you, then simply photocopy this page and use the following rules; that would be better than not using any rules. However, unless you have a personality that is almost identical to mine, chances are you won't be able to stick to this trading plan. Why? Because every person is unique, and every person needs his or her *own* trading plan. Remember, one of the hardest things about trading is knowing yourself.

Trading Plan

The following is a sample trading plan for beginning traders to adopt and modify as they see fit.

- Trades initiated will be trend reversal Gartley (TRG) Patterns that conform to the rules as set out in *The Gartley Trading Method*.

- Time frames for analysis will be the daily, 360-minute, and 45-minute charts.
- International equities, futures, and Forex markets will be scanned with the Market Analyst scanning feature set to find TRG786 patterns.
- Wolfe Wave lines will be drawn to confirm all TRG786 patterns.
- Trades will be executed with OptionsXpress directly off the chart with the OX plugin for Market Analyst.
- Risk on any one trade will not exceed 4 percent of trading capital available.
- In the event that my capital experiences a 50 percent drawdown, all positions will be liquidated, and no further trading will take place.
- New positions will always be in increments of three contracts, based on the single in/scale out rules of trade management as specified in the *Gartley Trading Method*. In the event that the risk of the three contracts exceeds the 4 percent rule, I will modify the size of the contract or not take the trade.
- The 3-bar trailing stop exit will always be used on the last third of the single in/scale out strategy.
- Stops will be in place at all times. I will enable audible alerts on Market Analyst to inform me of necessary order adjustments.
- After the setup criteria for the TRG786 is complete, entry will be based on the 1-bar reversal method.
- A chart of the instrument traded will be printed and kept in my trading journal. These charts will be kept for every entry and exit. In the event that there is a trade that creates a loss, I will fearlessly examine the trade to determine whether there was any way I can learn from it and improve this trading plan.
- I will not modify this plan with open positions on.
- Money used for trading will be risk capital.

A potential roadblock to sticking to a trading plan is the desire to change the plan and the rules in the middle of a trade. This is very typical of gamblers. To illustrate, imagine a gambler who visits Las Vegas with his wife for a weekend. He vows up and down that he will not lose more than $500 gambling over the weekend. You could call this his "trading plan." He starts playing blackjack, and by 9:00 P.M. Friday evening, he is down $1,000. What is he thinking now? "I have to win back at least $500 or my wife will kill me!" Typically, in this environment, the gambler will change his "system" and increase his risk, trying to get back to the $500 "stop loss" that he promised to his wife.

This "let's win it back" attitude often prevails in trading as well. When the trader deviates from his trading plan with open positions on, he is throwing caution to the wind, and it almost always results in tears. To avoid these pitfalls, it is imperative to write down our rules in our trading plan.

KEEPING A TRADING JOURNAL

After you complete your trading plan, you will need to start compiling a trading journal. The trading journal will give you a place to quantify your results and to determine whether your trading method is "working" or not. Once again, there may be resistance on the behalf of the general public to keep these results, especially if they are not good results. But remember, "Winners have simply formed the habit of doing things losers don't like to do." So be a "winner" and start compiling your results today; don't wait to do it when you are overwhelmed with the results of 50 trades.

I like easy, and the easiest way to keep a trading journal is to get a quality 3-hole punch, a 3-ring binder, a mechanical pencil, and a box of computer paper. If you have an inkjet printer, sell it and get a laser printer with a spare drum. At a minimum, simply print your charts every time an order is filled, then 3-hole punch the chart and put it in the binder. Use the mechanical pencil to make notations right on the chart. Make comments about the trade. Ask yourself who, what, when, where, and why, and write anything else that you think might help you. This could include what you ate, how much sleep you had, social issues, or that you missed yoga. Get some of those fancy colored tabs for your binder and sort each section by month. If you are a geek, use Excel and include hotlinks to .jpegs of your charts.

Next, 3-hole punch your trade confirmations and keep them beside your charts. When you receive your monthly statements, keep these together in a separate section of the binder. You will need these to calculate your monthly and annual rates of return. Also include your trading plan at the front of your trading journal binder; this will force you to remember your rules.

After a certain length of time, perhaps every quarter, every six months, or every year, plot a graph of your monthly returns after commissions and fees based on your monthly statements. Now calculate your annual rate of return. Compare your returns with benchmarks such as the S&P 500 Index or the Barclay's CTA Index. This exercise is crucial to trading longevity, because a reflection on your past results will remind you of the reliability of your trading method. Reflecting on past trading success can help you to keep going in the future after facing a temporary drawdown.

CONCLUSION

So, you made it! Congratulations, and I hope you enjoyed reading this book. I know some of you are still not willing to do what it takes, because it does require a lot of work. That is okay, I understand. Maybe you've spent a lot of time on some other endeavor and it didn't work out, and now you are "once bitten, twice shy." Therefore, I have personally created a software tool that you can use if you don't want to internalize all the information contained herein. This will rebuild your confidence; remember that some people actually make money trading. To learn more about the tools that I've made available for traders interested in trading Gartley patterns, go to www.geometrictrading.com.

Thanks for purchasing *The Gartley Trading Method*. My hope is that you will have found at least one helpful piece of advice that will make a difference in your trading. If the value of the book has exceeded the price that you paid for it, then please do me a favor; go to amazon.com and write a positive review for me. I hope to meet you one day (in this life, or the next), and I wish you future success in your trading endeavors.

APPENDIX A

Who Needs Elliott Wave?

In our noble quest for the "holy grail," many of us have tested every technical indicator under the sun. We quickly realize that there is limited value in the back-testing of multiple redundant indicators. Frustrated, we start to question the very existence of the grail itself. Then we hear the call of the siren—Elliott Wave. When we first hear of it, it seems to make perfect sense. The scales fall from our eyes as we begin to see patterns everywhere, because we have now received what R.N. Elliott referred to in his final book as *The Secret of the Universe*. It now appears that a trader can become the omniscient god of the markets with the ability to pinpoint every market turn.

To further support our newfound belief, we search the Internet to find that we are not alone. We find out that many others believe in Elliott Wave theory. But to truly reach the higher ranks of the "religion," we must purchase the automatic Elliott Wave software. At this point, if we were to complete a self-diagnosis, we would realize that we now have acquired Elliott Wave obsessive-compulsive disorder (EWOCD). Viewing it as a trading asset, we begin to trade with a slight doubt in our mind. "If other traders have obtained the grail, why are they so quick to tell still others about it? Is it not our duty as the keepers of the 'Secret of the Universe' to control this information?" After losing a significant amount of money trading Elliott Wave, we quickly realize that we are closer to being trading mortals than trading gods.

After reading *The Gartley Trading Method*, you may conclude that the Gartley Pattern replaces the Elliott Wave. The intent of this book is not to undermine the exhaustive technical work already accomplished by R.N. Elliott or Robert Prechter. I am truly grateful to have learned that the market does have a tendency to conform to Elliott Waves; however, we have to remember to be objective in our Elliott Wave analysis. It is not called Elliott Wave fact but Elliott Wave *theory*.

As scientists take sides in the argument between intelligent design and evolution, either belief is seen as an article of faith. Similarly, we must acknowledge that Elliott Wave theory is an article of faith as well. As mentioned, my intent is not to convince you to change your "religion" but rather to have an open mind and to be objective. It's funny how many trading gurus can achieve cult-like status with followers who refuse to ask questions. Blindly heeding the spiritual call of an Elliott Wave cult leader to sell in a bull market is about as smart as listening to Jim Jones in 1978. However, if I can't convince you to change your "religion" after reading this book, you should be happy to know that your Elliott Wave trades can be improved if you look for simple ABC corrections in the counter-trend move (more on this will follow). The Gartley Pattern can be used as a filter to help you achieve an Elliott Wave trade setup with even higher probability of success.

TRADE WAVE 1, 3, OR 5

It is important to note that if we simply look for TCGs or TRGs with an AB = CD, we will be identifying the end of Elliott Wave corrective phases, which will allow us to trade the impulse. In the three examples that follow, notice that Gartley Patterns allow us alternatively to trade Wave 1, 3, or 5.

Figure A.1 highlights a buy at the end of Wave 2 to trade Wave 3. A 78.6 percent retracement of Wave 1 can often resemble a double top or double bottom. Adding volume to the criteria of this setup would qualify this as a bullish TRG. Many Elliotticians will tell you that it is only at the end of Wave 4 that you should consider taking a trade. In other words, don't try to trade Wave 3 because you won't know that it's a Wave 3 until *after* it is complete. This is frustrating for Elliott traders who fantasize about trading Wave 3, because they know that it is typically the biggest wave.

Figure A.2 highlights a buy at the end of Wave 4 to trade Wave 5. This setup deviates from the original Gartley material in the sense that the picture on page 222 of *Profits in the Stock Market* displays an impulsive phase prior to the beginning of the

FIGURE A.1   End of Wave 2 and a Gartley

FIGURE A.2   End of Wave 4 and a Gartley

pattern. Therefore, this trade is a bullish TCG. The depth of the retracement level is often dependent on the strength of the trend. This setup is very common in the Elliott Wave world.

If you are going to continue using automated Elliott Wave software trade setups to trade Wave 5, do yourself a favor and add this one filter. Wait for Wave 4 to complete a simple ABC zigzag correction where Wave A and Wave C are approximately equal to each other. Using this filter requires patience, but it will keep you out of a lot of bad trades. A classic mistake with this trade is to enter with a tight stop and get stopped out; then the market immediately goes in the direction that you thought it would. These early Elliott traders often rely on a minimum 38.2 percent Fibonacci retracement of Wave 3 and a pullback to the zero line of the Elliott Oscillator (typically a 3.35 moving average crossover histogram) to enter a trade at what would appear to be the end of Wave 4. In reality, it is often only the completion of a Wave A of an ABC correction. These traders who get stopped out prematurely suffer from entry dysfunction (ED). The blue pill to remedy this ailment is to wait for Wave 4 to complete a simple ABC zigzag correction before entering.

Finally, have a look at Figure A.3. Waves 1 through 5 constitute the impulsive phase of a larger Gartley pattern followed by a larger ABC correction. As this example completes one cycle, we now enter our trade at the beginning of Wave 1.

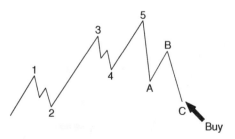

FIGURE A.3   End of Wave C and a Gartley

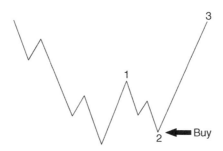

FIGURE A.4   Trading Wave 3

WAVE 3 OR C?

Have you ever executed a trade based on automatic Elliott Wave software wave counts only to have the software re-label the chart with an alternative wave count? How frustrating is that? Wouldn't it be nice if the chart would be re-labeled with an alternative Elliott Wave count and you could still make money? Do you like the idea of making money even when your wave count is wrong?

Have a look at Figure A.4. Ideally, this would be our dream trade—buy at the end of Wave 2 and trade Wave 3. Not only would we be trading in the direction of the trend (as signified by Wave 1), we would be trading what is typically the biggest wave, Wave 3.

However, what if we were wrong about this wave count? What if the next leg after we entered the market was a Wave C? That means we would be long and trading against the bearish trend. It also means that the market will eventually take out the previous low and go even lower. Our intent with the Gartley Pattern is not to trade counter trend, but even when we are wrong about our wave count, we can still make money.

How? Have a look at Figure A.5.

If we buy at the point suggested by Gartley at the end of Wave B, where should the market go before it makes a new low? It should go *up* to make a Wave C before it makes a new low. Therefore, Gartley's suggested entry point is a unique market position where

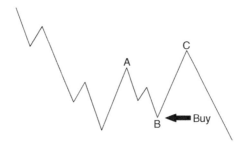

FIGURE A.5   Trading Wave C

the Elliott Wave count becomes irrelevant. It will turn into either a Wave 3 or a Wave C. This is the *ah-ha* moment for a lot of Elliott Wave traders. Once you start trading Gartleys, you really won't care what wave it is—Wave 3, 4, 5, 6, 7, or 8.

In view of the foregoing, it becomes apparent that if we simply look for Gartley Patterns, we will be trading Wave 1, 3, or 5. With that in mind we have to ask ourselves, "Who needs Elliott Wave?"

"Gann's"
Mysterious Emblem

I believe that the following information sheds some light on the meaning of the mysterious emblem on W.D. Gann's trading courses. For decades I've been under the false impression that the emblem of the connected circle, square, and triangle was a symbol developed by W.D. Gann. I learned the truth recently when I received a call from Cody Jones at Lambert-Gann publishing. After receiving this manuscript for review, Cody wanted me to know the "Gann" emblem was not Gann's invention, but his late father's, Billy Jones. According to Billy's wife Nikki, Billy and Nikki were in San Francisco in the 1970s and Billy noticed the peace sign buttons that were so common then. Using the peace sign symbol for inspiration, he combined the circle, square and triangle shapes into a logo to be used for the Lambert-Gann Publishing Company. I told Cody that maybe we should stop calling it Gann's emblem and give his dad credit and call it the Jones emblem!

If you haven't heard of W.D. Gann, he was one of the most famous stock and commodity traders of all time. For more information on W.D. Gann, check out www.wdgann.com. In the many years of applied technical trading, I have to admit that the methods that have worked most consistently for me are the methods discovered by W.D. Gann. Gann thought outside the box and was willing to be different. Being different and trying something new doesn't sit well with most people; however, to be an exceptional trader, you must keep an open mind. As German philosopher Arthur Schopenhauer stated, "All truth passes through three stages. First, it is ridiculed. Second, it is violently opposed. Third, it is accepted as being self-evident." In other words, when trying new trading techniques, you might want to keep them to yourself; otherwise don't be surprised to find yourself ridiculed. Sadly, those who ridicule you probably continue to lose money hand over fist with the same old tired indicators. What is the definition of insanity again?

I have spoken to many traders about Gann's successes, and opinions vary greatly. Some believe that he simply was a very skillful salesman who sold educational material. There is no doubt that Gann made money selling his courses, but the question is, Did he make money trading? I believe that he did for two reasons. The first is that there is more evidence that he was a successful trader than there is evidence to the contrary. The second reason is that of all the technical methods that I have used over the years, I keep coming back to the methods that Gann taught.

Rumor has it that Gann was a Mason, and because of that, geometry was very important to him, as it should be for all technical students of the financial markets. Why? Look at the shape of this book, the room you are sitting in, furniture, art, architecture, atoms—everything is geometry. We were created with a preference for symmetry, and we know that humans have a preference for order, proportion, symmetry, and balanced geometric shapes. Looking for geometry in the financial markets allows the technician to paint a picture of the future.

Circle, Square, and Triangle

The emblem found on W.D. Gann's published course materials consisted of the circle, the square, and the triangle; it is illustrated in Figure B.1.

In *The Basis of My Forecasting Method*, W.D. Gann stated,

> No matter whether you use geometry, trigonometry, or calculus, you use the simple rules of arithmetic. You do only two things, you increase or decrease. There are two kinds of numbers, odd and even. We add numbers together, which is increasing. We multiply, which is a shorter way to increase. We subtract, which decreases, and we divide, which also decreases. With the use of higher mathematics, we find a quicker and easier way to divide, subtract, add, and multiply, yet very simple when you understand it. Everything in nature is male and female,

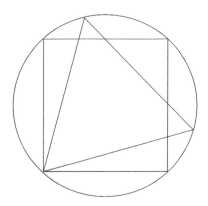

FIGURE B.1 "Gann's" Emblem

white and black, harmony or in harmony, right and left. The market moves only two ways, up and down. There are three dimensions which we know how to prove—width, length, and height. We use three figures in geometry—the circle, the square, and the triangle. We get the square and triangle points of a circle to determine points of time, price, and space resistance. We use the circle of 360 degrees to measure Time and Price. There are three kinds of angles—the vertical, the horizontal, and the diagonal, which we use for measuring time and price movements.

The mysterious "Gann" emblem is most often described by Gann educators as a calendar overlay on Gann's square of 9 calculators. Without delving too deep into the symbolism behind the field of sacred geometry, most students of it would recognize that the circle represents one complete cycle. The triangle of "Gann's" emblem was inside of the circle and this divided the cycle into thirds. A square was also within the circle and this represented dividing the cycle into quarters and halves. From these three primary geometric forms are derived the following number sequence, 1, .75, .66, .5, .33, .25. Some Gann traders also use these numbers as support and resistance levels in the same fashion that we have used Fibonacci ratios for retracement levels.

Timing Is Everything

Gann was known for putting great emphasis on the timing element of his trades, as he mentioned in the paragraph quoted. Some of the most important filters that I have discovered that improve the reliability of the Gartley Pattern have to do with time analysis. Time analysis is largely ignored by many in the technical community, yet these same individuals will insist that a trendline is a useful tool. Unwittingly they are using time analysis, inasmuch as any line that is not purely horizontal incorporates the y and x axes. A diagonal line such as a trendline includes *both* price and time.

Until recently, I looked only for Gartley Patterns based on horizontal price lines, such as the price-extension and retracement lines. I was often asked by students if there was any relationship between the slope of the X–A leg and the completion of a Gartley at the D point. My answer was usually based on Larry Pesavento's observation in *Fibonacci Ratios with Pattern Recognition*, where he states that there is a proportional relationship between the X–A leg and the A–D move. I would argue that since the ABDC move is a correction against the trend (X–A), corrections usually happen in a shorter period of time than the trend movement. In other words, my ideal Gartley was one where the number of bars in the A–D move would be less than those in the X–A move. To confirm this, I would use Gann squares to check this timing element as a filter for valid Gartley Patterns.

However, the problem would often arise where there was a perfect Gartley Pattern that would complete beyond the 100 percent time retracement of the X–A leg.

This bothered me for over 10 years, but the scales fell from my eyes when I began digging into some of the material of Michael S. Jenkins. Michael is an expert market geometer and an authority on the techniques of W.D. Gann. After reading Michael's material, it became apparent to me that much of the Gann material being taught was accurate except for one vital piece of information—*offset angles.* Thereafter, I started to combine the market geometry of W.D. Gann and Billy Jones with my Gartley analysis. I discovered that the slope and length of the X–A move had amazing forecasting value.

Offset Angles

Many traders are familiar with the "Gann Fan." The chart is treated like a square, and a line is drawn on the diagonal of the square to divide it in half. Gann referred to this as the 1X1 angle. Additional fractions of these two triangles are derived by adding additional angles, as displayed in Figure B.2.

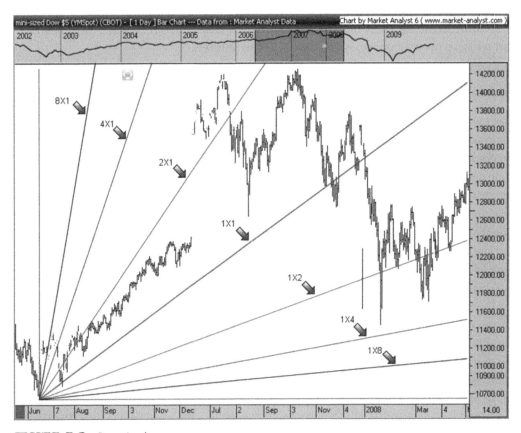

FIGURE B.2 Gann Angles

As many traders are aware, the Gann Fan typically requires an input as to how many units of time are required for each unit of price. Calculating this ratio is the difficult part of using the Gann angles in the traditional manner. This was not an issue when traders used large paper charts. However, now that we trade off of computer screens, it is a simple function to squeeze many bars of data onto a screen with the click of a mouse. Each time we do this, we are altering the ratio between time and price. In exchange for this convenience, most traders disregard Gann price- and time-squaring techniques. However, I believe that the geometry found in the relationship between time and price is still the key to forecasting the financial markets.

When we draw geometric shapes on a screen-based chart and the time and price scaling is not locked, we risk turning our circles into ellipses and our squares into rectangles by squeezing more price data onto the screen. This appears to be one of the major issues of the modern market geometer. Conversely, paper charts have "locked" the price and time ratios. Therefore, there is an advantage to using paper charts for market geometry. If you have access to a drafting table with a large plotter/printer that is capable of printing huge charts, you will have an advantage over the trader with a 14-inch screen who keeps rescaling his chart.

Also, looking for a time and price ratio from data that is 100 years old and using that ratio to predict what is going to happen in the market today doesn't make sense. Why? You shouldn't expect the psychology of dead people to be reflected in today's market action. Current market data reflects the psychology of the current participants. The farther we go back in time to calculate a price-and-time ratio, the further away we are from the psychology of the current market participants.

Is there a better way of calculating the correct price-and-time ratio of the current market participants? Yes; simply draw the 1X1 line yourself on the uptrend as shown in Figure B.3; this recent market action gives you a better idea of the most current relationship between price and time.

Notice the difference between the results of the previous two charts in Figures B.2 and B.3. When we draw the 1X1 line ourselves on the second chart, the picture is much clearer. The idea behind the fan lines is that they act as support and resistance lines, just like Fibonacci lines. Notice that after a line from the June 2006 low up to the October 2007 high in Figure B.3 was drawn, the Dow declined and bounced off of the 1X2 line. Once there was a significant break below the 1X2 line, the market found support at the 1X4 line. Angles identify more accurate support and resistance levels when you draw a 1X1 line yourself rather than using a predetermined price-and-time ratio based on historical data that may no longer be valid.

The benefit in using angles for support and resistance instead of the standard horizontal support and resistance lines is that angles reflect support and resistance in price *and* time.

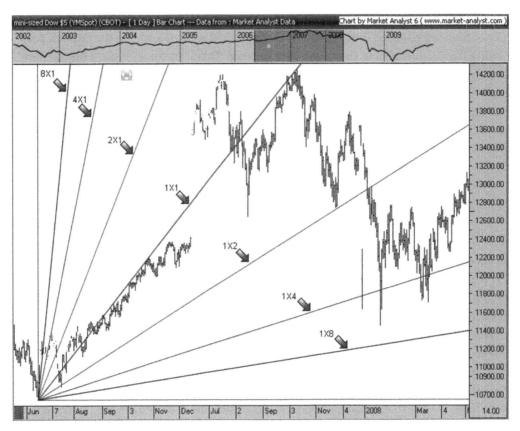

FIGURE B.3 Offset Angles

Beck's Emblem

After trying to figure out how angles, circles, squares, and triangles relate to the Gartley pattern, it dawned on me that "Gann's" emblem fits perfectly right on top of an XABCD Gartley. One way to do this would be to line up the left side of the square with the left side of our chart. However, if we choose this option, we still run into the same problem that we had with the Gann angles in Figure B.2. The angles in Figure B.2 were simply lining up with the side of our chart, regardless of how much data we had on the screen. To avoid the scaling issue, let's line up the left side of the square with a significant high and low, such as the X–A leg in the Gartley Pattern. Notice in Figure B.4 how the arrow is pointing to the side of the square line that we need to line up with the X–A leg.

Once we have drawn the line between the two data points (X–A), we are able to draw the square of "Gann's" emblem. After the square is complete, we can draw the circle and the triangle. Here is where it gets interesting. If we intend to use this offset symbol to

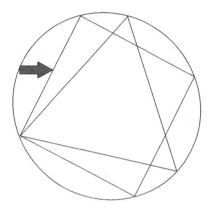

FIGURE B.4 "Gann" Emblem Offset

find additional angles for support and resistance, we will draw another triangle as shown in Figure B.5.

The next step is to draw the final triangle as seen in Figure B.6. This gives us what I call Beck's Emblem.

The implications of the relationship between the Gartley Pattern and Beck's Emblem are numerous. One question that could be raised is, "Do the price/time angles of Beck's Emblem replace traditional horizontal Fibonacci lines?" I'm sorry, but you will need to wait; the answer to that question will appear in my next book.

If you want to use the good old compass and straightedge of Euclidean geometry, you can trade just like the masters of old such as H.M. Gartley and W.D. Gann using Beck's Emblem. Let's see how we can draw the emblem on a chart with some basic drawing tools found in most technical analysis software programs.

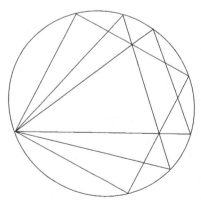

FIGURE B.5 Offset Emblem with Two Triangles

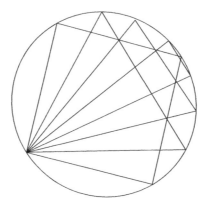

FIGURE B.6   Beck's Emblem

TCG EXAMPLE WITH BECK'S EMBLEM

The first wave of a five-wave sequence has tremendous forecasting value for the remaining waves that come out of this initial thrust. This is the "seed" or beginning of a geometric structure of growth. Following this "seed" is the typical Elliott ABC zigzag correction.

The first step in constructing Beck's Emblem is to identify the impulse phase (X–A) of the Gartley Pattern and draw a trendline from the low to the high or the high to the low. In the example shown in Figure B.7, we are drawing a geometric trendline from the high to the low. This line is the most important part of Beck's Emblem.

Once we draw a line from the beginning to the end of the impulsive phase, we are able to draw a square. In Market Analyst, you first need to draw a geometric line (not a trendline) on the impulse, then right click; under Actions, choose Make Square. This action is shown in Figure B.8.

We now have to find the center of the square so that we can draw a circle around it. Draw trend lines in the square to find the middle point, as shown in Figure B.9.

With the middle point established, we can now draw a geometric circle. To do this, click the center of the square where the trendlines cross each other and click one of the edges of the square. This should draw a circle that connects with each corner of the square, as shown in Figure B.10.

Next, we need to draw another circle. This circle must be drawn in the direction of the X–A leg. The arrows in the example in Figure B.11 show you where to click on the chart to draw the second circle. The first click is at the arrow on the right, and the next click is at the arrow on the left.

Now we draw a trendline between the two points where the circles intersect, as highlighted with the two arrows on the chart in Figure B.12.

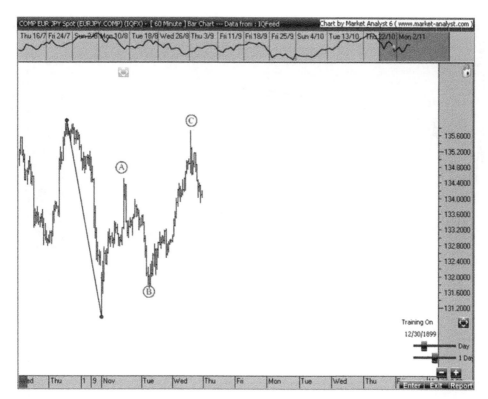

FIGURE B.7 Identify the "Seed" with Trendline

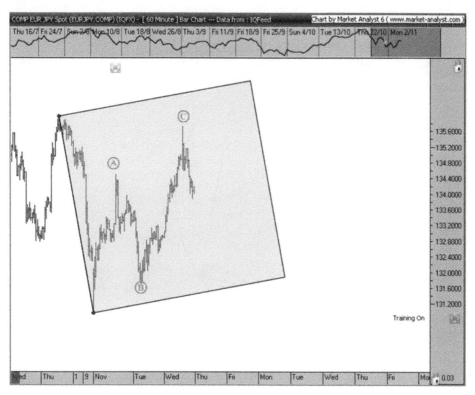

FIGURE B.8 Draw a Square

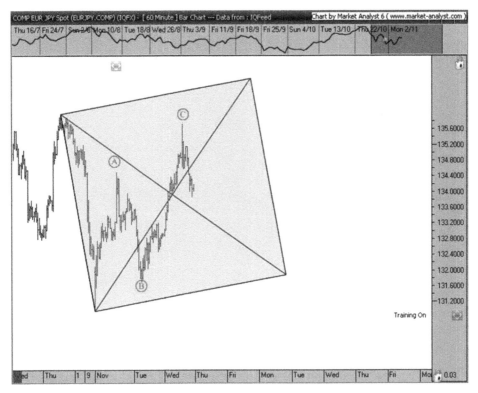

FIGURE B.9 Draw Trend Lines to Find Center

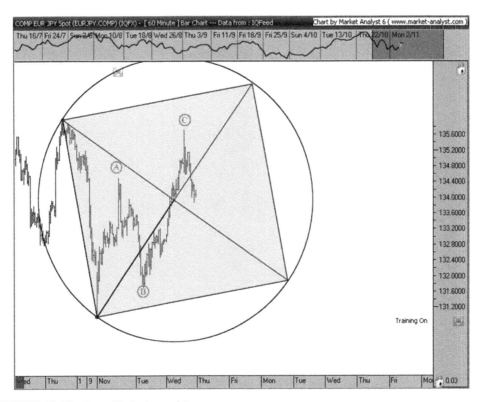

FIGURE B.10 Draw Circle Around Square

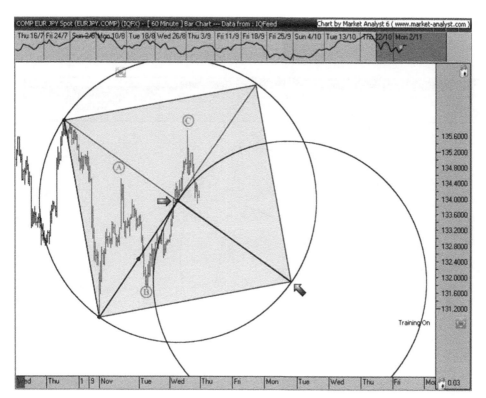

FIGURE B.11 Draw Second Circle

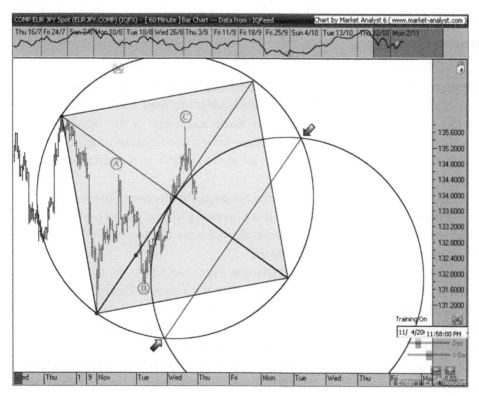

FIGURE B.12 Trendline in the "Almond"

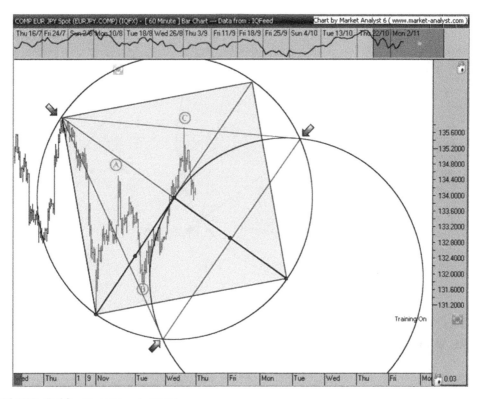

FIGURE B.13   First Triangle Visible

Students of sacred geometry will recognize the intersection of these two circles as the "Vesica Pisces" which literally means "the bladder of a fish." It is also a yonic symbol (look that one up!). The ratio between the width and length of this mandorla (Italian for almond) is the square root of 3. Now if we draw a line from the origin of the impulsive phase to the two ends of the almond, we should be able to recognize an equilateral triangle, as shown in Figure B.13.

In Figure B.13 we have now completed the geometry necessary to see "Gann's" emblem of the circle, square, and triangle. It is interesting to note that in order to draw the triangle, we had to draw the Vesica Pisces. We will leave the second circle on the chart as we continue to complete Beck's emblem.

Now we need to draw the second triangle. First, find where the triangle intersects with the lower-right quadrant of the square inside the Vesica in Figure B.14. Next draw two lines from the origin of the impulsive phase through these intersections to the edge of the first circle. Next, draw a trendline between the two end points of these trendlines to complete the second triangle, as shown in Figure B.14.

Finally, we will draw the last triangle. Find where the triangle intersects with the square inside the Vesica. Then draw trendlines from the origin of the impulsive phase,

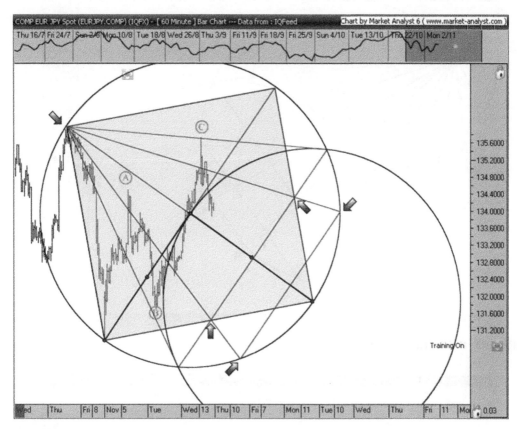

FIGURE B.14 Second Triangle

through the intersections, to the edge of the first circle. Complete the triangle by drawing a trendline between the two end points of the lines. You should now be able to identify Beck's Emblem, as shown in Figure B.15.

Now we have completed the necessary calculations for the proper triangles derived from the initial impulse. We are interested only in the triangle lines that will intersect with our quadrilateral tool. Now use the quadrilateral to tool to determine point D (end of Wave C).

In Figure B.16, we have drawn a quadrilateral as our price projection. As you can see, the tip of the quadrilateral is closest to the second triangle. The quadrilateral tells us that the reversal should be taking place at the triangle line to which it lands closest. In this case, the upper side of the second triangle will be our sell signal.

The diagonal line of our second triangle is an improvement over using a simple price retracement. Remember that diagonal lines such as trendlines have a timing element. The angle of the impulse (X–A) tells us how deep the retracement will be in price and how long a correction should take in time. The correction of the bearish TCG should

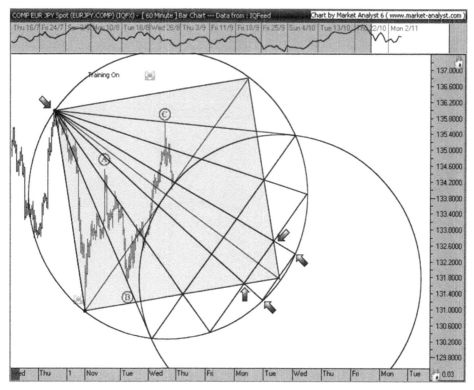

FIGURE B.15 Third Triangle

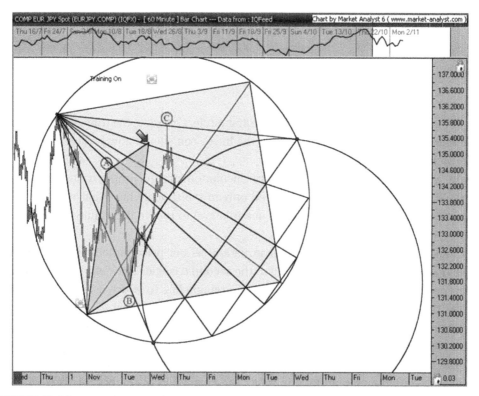

FIGURE B.16 Draw the Quadrilateral

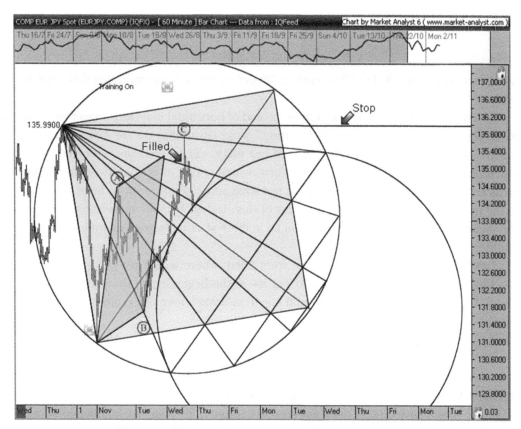

FIGURE B.17 Protective Buy Stop

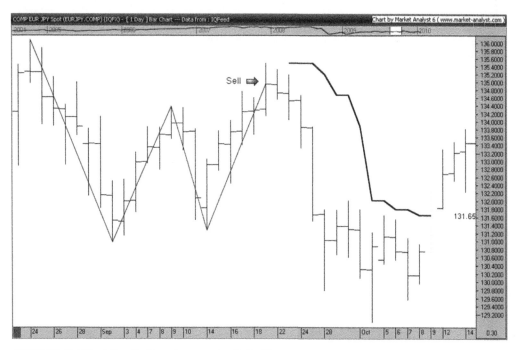

FIGURE B.18 3-Bar Trailing Stop on the Daily Chart

take place within the circle of the emblem. Therefore, there is an expiration date on this trade.

The downside of using diagonal lines instead of horizontal lines as a trigger to enter a market is that it requires more "babysitting." Why? Given that we are looking at a 60-minute chart, this means that the price of our entry will be changing every hour. As our triangle line is sloping down, that means that the price of our limit orders will be reduced every 60 minutes. I know this is not what some of you want to hear, but I am in the process of having the execution part of this strategy become more automated. In the meantime, if your software gives you an audible alert on a trendline, then use that feature.

Getting back to our example, if we were filled, where would we put our stop? In the same place that Gartley tells us to put it—at the beginning of the pattern (X). In Figure B.17, I have displayed a horizontal line to indicate where our protective buy stop should be placed.

As you can see in Figure B.17, we were filled at T2 (triangle 2). After our fill, the market declined enough to hit both of the targets of the single in/scale out strategy. Next, we would change our time frame from the 60-minute chart to the daily chart. In the chart in Figure B.18, we have applied the 3-bar trailing stop to the daily chart at the point at which we would have bought back our second contract. The resulting liquidation of our final contract based on the 3-bar trailing stop can be seen in Figure B.18.

Wolfe Wave

There is no end to the different technical methods that you can use to filter your Gartley trades further. One of the best techniques that lends itself well to the Gartley Pattern is the Wolfe Wave. The Wolfe Wave was developed by Bill Wolfe at wolfewave.com. It can be used as an additional filter to help us identify the D point of a Gartley Pattern.

The first step is to find a five-wave Elliott Wave sequence that is part of the X–A move. The next step is to identify the end of Wave 4 within the five-wave sequence. In the USD/JPY chart shown in Figure C.1 we have a bullish TRG786, and we have labeled the X–A move with a five-wave count followed by the ABC labeling of the A–D move. If you label your Gartley Pattern as we have here, always make sure that Wave A is below Wave 4; if it isn't, you can't use the Wolfe Wave.

The next step is to draw a trendline from the end of Wave 4 to the end of Wave A (point B of the XABCD labeling). Make sure that your trendline drawing tool is not set to drawing a line segment; instead, it needs to extend to the right. The result appears in Figure C.2.

Notice how the Wolfe Wave identified support at the completion of the bullish TRG786? The convergence of the tip of our quadrilateral, the price retracement line, and the Wolfe Wave line have identified a narrow band of price and time for our TRG786 to complete.

Let's look at another example involving the USD/CAD in Figure C.3. We have labeled the chart, and it looks as though we have a potential bearish TCG786. Can we use the Wolfe Wave? Just by eyeballing the chart, you should be able to answer Yes.

Now let's draw a trendline from the end of Wave 4 to the end of Wave A (point B of the XABCD labeling). As you can see in Figure C.4, the market reversed within a few

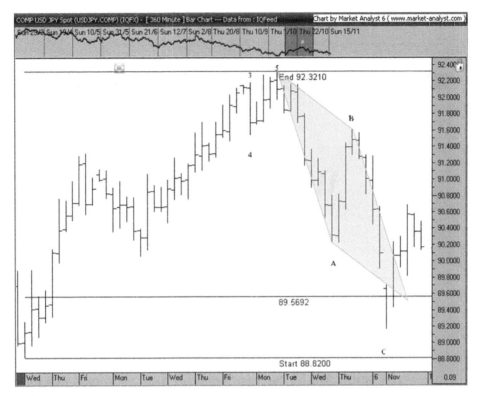

FIGURE C.1 USD/JPY Bullish TRG786

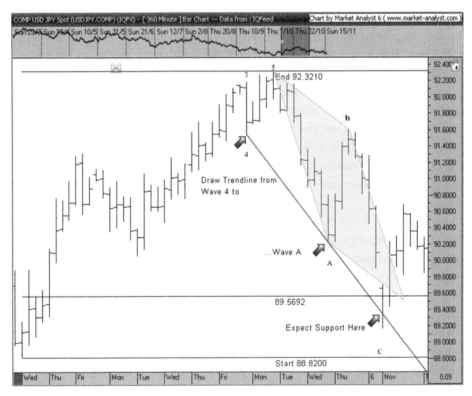

FIGURE C.2 USD/JPY Bullish TRG786 with Wolfe Wave

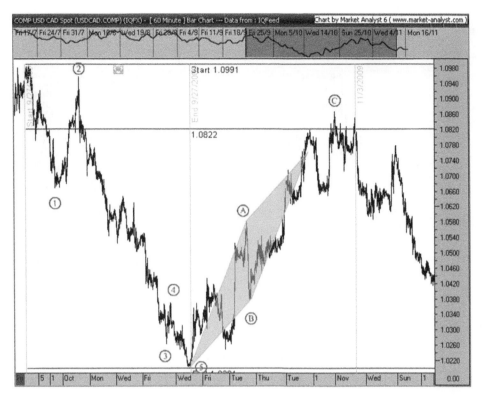

FIGURE C.3 USD/CAD Bearish TCG786

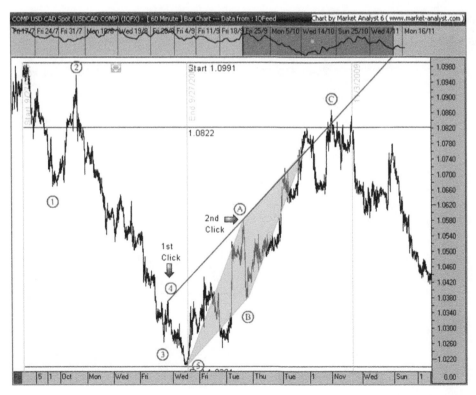

FIGURE C.4 USD/CAD Bearish TCG786 with Wolfe Wave

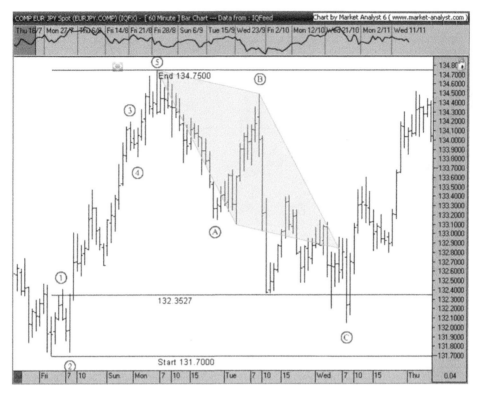

FIGURE C.5 EUR/JPY Bullish TCG786

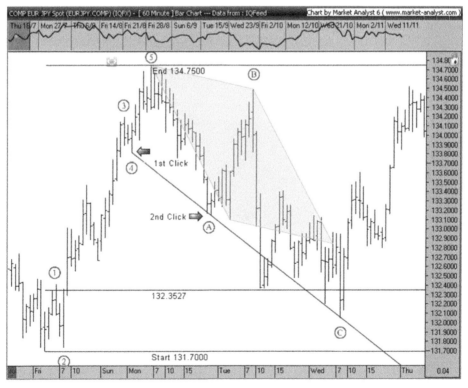

FIGURE C.6 EUR/JPY Bullish TCG786 with Wolfe Wave

hours of the intersection of our Wolfe Wave line and the 78.6 percent retracement line at 1.0822.

Here is one last example. We have a bullish TCG786 with the Wolfe Wave on a 60-minute EUR/JPY chart. The chart in Figure C.5 already has the Elliott Wave labels applied for us. Do you remember how to draw the Wolfe Wave trendline?

Draw the line between the end of Wave 4 and the end of Wave A. As you can see in Figure C.6, the EUR/JPY found support at our Wolfe Wave line as expected.

The low at the end of Wave C was made exactly on the Wolfe Wave line. Also notice in Figure C.6 how the contribution of time analysis from the quadrilateral told us that a low was imminent.

Students often ask, "Will you trade a Gartley without a Wolfe Wave being present?" The answer is Yes. However, if there are two Gartley patterns that look similar and you have to make a decision between the two, look to see whether there is a Wolfe Wave present on one of the charts. If so, choose the Gartley Pattern with the Wolfe Wave.

Glossary

A

AB = CD   A label created by Larry Pesavento based on page 249 of H.M. Gartley's book *Profits in the Stock Market*.

ABC Zigzag   R.N. Elliott's term for a simple corrective phase.

Advantage Gambling   Using legal ways to gain a mathematical advantage while gambling. Poker is an example of advantage gambling; players with the most skill usually win.

Alchemy   From the Arabic *Al-kimi*. Attempting to turn base metals into gold in a physical or philosophical sense.

Alternative Elliott Wave Count   The way an Elliott Wave guru can always be "right."

Arithmetic Scaling   Equidistant price intervals on the y axis of a price chart.

B

Bearish   Expecting market weakness.

Beck's Emblem   The Gann emblem of circle, square, and triangle with two additional triangles added. The triangle lines are used to determine support and resistance levels.

Black Box   A trading system, which is available for purchase, that generates trading signals. The "secret" as to how the signals are generated is known only by the vendor.

Bullish   Describing the optimism the investing public feels during a period of share price strength.

C

Calendar Day Charts   Charts that include spaces for "weekend trading." Useful for time analysis.

Candlestick Entry Method   Using a Japanese candlestick formation to enter the market at the completion of a Gartley Pattern.

Cluster   When price and time projections land close to each other or converge.

Continuous Chart   A futures chart that combines expiring contract months to create a longer term chart.

Contract   A trading unit of a derivative product.

Contracting Geometric Series   1.00, .786, .618, .486, .382. A series introduced to the trading world by Bryce Gilmore in *Geometry of the Markets II*.

Corrective Phase   The term used by R.N. Elliott to describe a counter trend—typically three waves.

Counter Trend   A temporary movement against the underlying direction of the market.

CTA   Commodity Trading Advisor. A registration category as defined by the National Futures Association.

D

Day Trader   A trader who typically trades off of intraday data and doesn't hold positions overnight.

Derivatives   Financial instruments or contracts *derived* from another asset. Futures and options are examples of derivatives.

Divination   Attempting to foretell the future through contact with a supernatural agency.

Double Top/Double Bottom   A chart formation where there is a retest of a previous high or low.

Drawdown   The decline in value of a trading account measured from the most recent equity high.

Dynamic   From the Greek word for power. Further definition relates to objects in motion and continuous change. The opposite of static.

E

ED   Entry dysfunction. Entering a position and getting stopped out, only to watch the market move in the direction that you thought it would.

Ego   Greek for "I." A person's ego is the biggest obstacle to trading success.

Elliott, R.N.   Technical analyst who wrote *The Wave Principle* in 1938 and father of Elliott Wave theory.

Elliott Wave   A theory that future movements in the financial markets are predictable based on a repetitive series of waves. Trends are 5-wave structures and counter trends are typically 3-wave structures.

Entry   Opening a position, not to be confused with a setup.

EWOCD   Elliott Wave obsessive compulsive disorder. A trader who has a need to label every chart he sees with Elliott Wave labels.

Exit   Closing an open position.

F

Fib   Abbreviation of Fibonacci.

Fibonacci   Name of an Italian mathematician from the 13th century who identified a series of numbers that relate to each other by the golden ratio of 1.618.

Fibonacci Entry Method   Using the price indicated by a Fibonacci ratio to enter the market at the completion of a Gartley Pattern.

Financial Pornography   Sensational advertising of trading systems.

Fundamental Analysis   Using information about such things as the economy, interest rates, production, and earnings to determine the future price action of a financial instrument.

Futures   Financial instruments that are valued based on a future price.

G

G222   The term used by Larry Pesavento for the Gartley Pattern. The picture of the pattern appears on page 222 of Gartley's book *Profits in the Stock Market.*

Gambling   Placing a wager on an uncertain event that has a monetary outcome within a limited period of time.

Gann Box   A drawing tool that creates a box with user-defined time and price ratios. Angles within the box identify support and resistance levels.

Gann Emblem   A circle with a square and a triangle inside of it. Invented by Billy Jones.

Gann Fan   A drawing tool that creates a fan of angles that originate at a user-defined high or low. Angle lines identify support and resistance levels.

Gann, W.D.   Legendary stock and commodity trader (1878–1955), author, and educator. Used natural law and geometric proportion to identify trading opportunities.

Gartley, H.M.   Prominent Wall Street technician (1899–1972) and author of *Profits in the Stock Market.*

Gartley Pattern   Pattern based on what H.M. Gartley described as "One of the Best Trading Opportunities" on pages 221 and 222 of his book *Profits in the Stock Market.*

H

Harami   A Japanese candlestick pattern. Harami means "pregnant" in Japanese.

Head and Shoulders   A chart formation that resembles a head and two shoulders.

Hobby   An activity that generates a negative rate of return.

Hopium   The figurative product that a trader smokes, and is stupefied by, when he keeps holding a bad position and "hopes" that it will work.

Holy Grail   A mechanical trading system that never loses and imparts everlasting life (in the financial markets) to the trader that finds it.

I

Impulsive Phase   The term used by R.N. Elliott to describe a trend, typically one having five waves.

Indicator   A mathematical calculation of historical prices to predict future prices. Usually displayed as a colorful squiggly line on the bottom of the chart. Provides limited forecasting value.

Inside Bar   A price bar whose range is within or inside the range of the bar that immediately precedes it.

J

Japanese Candlesticks   A method of drawing price data on a chart. Each candlestick is equivalent to a bar of data and represents the open, high, low, and close with an emphasis between the opening and closing prices.

L

Labeling Using letters on a price chart to identify specific waves, legs, or swings of a price pattern.

Lagging Indicator An indicator that confirms the direction of the market after the fact.

Leading Indicator An indicator that predicts the direction of the market in advance.

Limit An order to buy or sell at a specific price that is better than the current price.

Liquidate To close out open positions.

Logarithmic Scaling A scale that uses the logarithm of a quantity instead of the quantity itself. For example equally spaced divisions on the price axis of a chart are labeled as 1, 10, 100, 1,000, instead of 1, 2, 3, 4.

Long Term to describe a trader's open position after purchasing a financial product.

Loser A word that novice traders use to describe themselves after a liquidating a losing position. Professionals don't take trading losses personally.

Lot One contract.

Lottery Ticket Contract The last contract of the single in/scale out strategy.

M

Mandorla Italian for almond. Used to describe the intersection of the two circles used to draw Gann's emblem and Beck's emblem.

Market Analyst Advanced technical analysis software developed in Australia.

Martingale A gambling system that doubles a bet after every loss so that when there is a win, all losses are won back, along with the amount of the initial bet.

Mechanical A style of entering orders in the financial markets based on a predetermined set of criteria, rather than emotion.

Mirage Seeing a trade opportunity that doesn't exist.

N

Nausea The feelings often associated with liquidating losing positions. This negative reaction causes novice traders to avoid learning how to improve their exit strategies.

NFA National Futures Association—the self-regulatory organization for the U.S. futures industry

O

Objective Based on reality, not influenced by personal perspective. Opposite of subjective.

Offset Angles Drawing angles on a chart based on the current slope of the trend as opposed to a historical price and time ratio.

One-Bar Reversal Entry Method Using the low (for short trades) or high (for long trades) of the previous bar to enter the market at the completion of a Gartley Pattern.

Oscillator A trend indicator that oscillates above and below a zero line. Used to identify overbought and oversold conditions.

OHLC   A bar of price data that represents open, high, low, and close prices.

Ordo ab Chao   Latin for "Out of chaos comes order." An axiom of the fraternity of Masons and a reminder that a price chart initially looks like chaos until we look for symmetry, geometry, and proportion.

Overbalance   W.D. Gann discussed the overbalance of price and time. For example, an overbalance of price would occur if the current rally exceeds the range on the previous rallies in a bear market.

P

Pesavento, Larry   Trading author and educator from Tucson, AZ. The first to coin the terms Gartley Pattern and G222.

Philosophers' Stone   Mentioned by H.M. Gartley on page 1 of *Profits in the Stock Market*. The legendary substance of alchemy that allows the user to turn base metals to gold.

Position Trader   A trader that typically holds a position or an open trade for weeks to months and sometimes years.

Price Extension   A drawing tool that compares the proportional relationships between two legs on a price chart that are moving in the same direction.

Price Retracement   A drawing tool that compares the proportional relationships between a trend leg and its connecting counter-trend leg.

Professional   A person who performs commercially in a field typically reserved for hobbyists or amateurs. This word is a reminder that if you treat trading as a hobby, it will pay you as a hobby. Treat trading as a profession.

Pulling the Trigger   Entering a position in the financial markets.

Q

Quadrilateral   A polygon with four sides. Used as a price-extension drawing tool.

R

Risk Management   An often overlooked subject that could be the real holy grail of trading.

S

Sacred Geometry   A belief that geometry is found in everything. Typically found in nature, religious art and architecture, but also appears on price charts of financial markets.

Scale   Measurement based on a numerical sequence.

Scale In/Single Out   Entering a market at intervals of varying degrees and liquidating them at a single price for a profit. A Martingale with a cap.

SEC   Securities and Exchange Commission. The mission of the U.S. Securities and Exchange Commission is to protect investors; maintain fair, orderly, and efficient markets; and facilitate capital formation.

Setup When the trade criteria of a trading plan is fulfilled. The setup is the precursor to order entry.

Short Term to describe a trader's open position after selling a financial product with the intent of buying it back later for a profit.

Single In/Scale Out Entering a market with multiple contracts at the same price and liquidating them at intervals of varying length.

Software Computer code written by imperfect humans. Software can help a trader make a decision, but it should never *make* the decision. "Black box" trading systems that generate automatic trading signals exemplify how decision making is taken away from the individual.

Spot Cash market.

Square-Root Scaling A scale that uses the square root of a quantity instead of the quantity itself. For example equally spaced divisions on the price axis of a chart are labeled as 1, 4, 9, 16, instead of 1, 2, 3, 4.

Static Unable or unwilling to change.

Stochastic Oscillator Momentum indicator developed by Dr. George Lane in the 1950s.

Stop Order An order to liquidate a position at the market if the market trades at the stop price.

Subjective Personal perspective. Elliott Wave is a subjective technical method.

Swing Chart Overlay An indicator that draws a line between the extreme highs and lows of a price chart.

Swing Trader A trader who typically holds a position from a few days to a few weeks.

T

TCG Trend-continuation Gartley Pattern. A new acronym to describe a Gartley Pattern that completes once a trend has already been established.

Technical Analysis Using historical price data to determine future price action.

Technical Indicator Entry Method Using a technical indicator to enter the market at the completion of a Gartley Pattern.

Three-Bar Trailing Stop A trailing stop that uses the highest high (short trades) or the lowest low (long trades) of the previous three bars (except inside bars) as the location for a protective stop order.

Trading Journal A journal of trading results. The journal should include charts with exact entry and exit points and a specific profit or loss result.

Trading Plan The "mission statement" of a trader. This includes not just the trader's philosophy but his rules.

Trading System A method of trading that typically is computer or software dependent and developed for private use or for sale. Some are fully disclosed, and some are "black boxes."

Trailing Stop A stop order that is moved incrementally in the direction of a profitable trade.

Trend   A significant directional move in the financial markets that typically conforms to the rules of an Elliott Wave impulsive phase.

Trendline   A line drawn on a price chart that is typically diagonal. Identifies trends and trend reversals.

TRG   Trend-reversal Gartley Pattern. A new acronym to describe a Gartley Pattern that completes when a trend is reversing.

V

Vesica Pisces   Literally, "bladder of a fish" in Latin. The intersection of two circles of the same radius.

Volume   An indicator that displays the number of transactions that take place on an exchange.

W

Weekend Trading   Trading decisions that are made on the weekends but are not executed until exchanges are physically open.

White Space   Right side of the chart, the future. The technician's canvas.

Wolfe Wave   A method to determine the end of a corrective phase developed by Bill Wolfe. For more information, go to wolfewave.com

W–X   A new label that identifies the leg prior to the XABCD pattern.

X

X Axis   The horizontal axis displaying time on a price chart.

Y

Y Axis   The vertical axis displaying price on a price chart.

Z

Zigzag Indicator   An indicator that draws a line between the extreme highs and lows of a price chart.

Bibliography

Carney, Scott. *Harmonic Trading, Volume One: Profiting from the Natural Order of the Financial Markets*. Upper Saddle River, NJ: FT Press, 2010.

Elliott, R.N. *R.N. Elliott's Masterworks: The Definitive Collection*. Gainesville, GA: New Classics Library, 2004.

Gann, W.D. *The Basis of My Forecasting Method*, self-published, 1935.

———. *The Magic Word*. Pomeroy, WA: Lambert-Gann Publishing, 1950.

Garrett, W.C. *Investing for Profit with Torque Analysis of Stock Market Cycles*. Cedar Falls, IA: Traders Press, 2000, p. 242.

Gartley, H.M. *Profits in the Stock Market*. Pomeroy, WA: Lambert-Gann Publishing, 1935.

Gilmore, Bryce T. *Geometry of the Markets II*, self-published, 1993.

Hurst, J.M. *The Profit Magic of Stock Transaction Timing*. Cedar Falls, IA: Traders Press, 2000.

Jenkins, Michael S. *The Secret Science of the Stock Market*. New York: Stock Cycles Forecast, 2004.

LeFevre, Edwin. *Reminiscences of a Stock Operator*. Hoboken, NJ: John Wiley & Sons, 2004, p. 83.

Lindsay, Charles L. *Trident: A Trading Strategy*. Brightwater, NY: Windsor Books, 1991.

Miner, Robert C. *Dynamic Trading: Dynamic Concepts in Time, Price & Pattern Analysis with Practical Strategies for Traders & Investors*. Cedar Falls, IA: Traders Press, 2002.

Pesavento, Larry. *Astro Cycles: The Traders Viewpoint*. Cedar Falls, IA: Traders Press, 1997.

———. *Fibonacci Ratios with Pattern Recognition*. Cedar Falls, IA: Traders Press, 1997.

———. *Planetary Harmonics of Speculative Markets*. Cedar Falls, IA: Traders Press, 1996.

The Market Analyst Beck Toolkit

Market Analyst International Pty Ltd (MA) is an Australian company based in Brisbane, Australia. I recently traveled to Australia to visit Mathew Verdouw and his team. I have to admit that I've never seen a group of individuals so passionate about providing cutting-edge technology to market technicians. If you haven't yet seen the technology that Tom Cruise was using in the movie *Minority Report* applied to technical analysis, stay tuned!

The programmers at MA were kind enough to create the Beck Toolkit for me. The Market Analyst Beck Toolkit includes the following tools:

- Beck's Emblem.
- Gartley Pattern Identifier.
- Gartley Pattern Scanner.
- X Bar Trailing Stop.
- Single In/Scale Out Profit and Stop Levels.

Rather than drawing Beck's emblem as we did in Appendix B, the toolkit from Market Analyst draws it with two clicks. In addition, the Gartley Pattern Identifier searches for TCGs and TRGs, including the W–X leg.

For a free trial of Market Analyst Software with the Beck Toolkit, go to www.geometrictrading.com.

About the Author

Ross Beck, FCSI, is a world-renowned public speaker on the subject of technical analysis and has written for numerous trading publications. As the recognized authority on the subject of the Gartley Pattern, Ross has been consulted by a number of technical analysis software companies to assist them in the creation of Gartley Pattern functionality. Ross is a member of the Market Technicians Association, a DMS (Derivatives Market Specialist), and an FCSI (Fellow of the Canadian Securities Institute). The FCSI designation is the top award offered by the Canadian Securities Institute and is reserved solely for professionals who meet the highest standards for education, ethics, and industry experience.

Ross is an avid student of history, music, philosophy, and religion. He lives with his wife Lindsay in Point Roberts, Washington, with their two cats, Lily and Sabbath.

Index

Printed and bound by CPI Group (UK) Ltd, Croydon, CR0 4YY

16/04/2025

14658509-0003